West Highland Way

Also available:
Capital Ring
The London Loop
The Coast to Coast Walk

West Highland Way

Anthony Burton

Photographs by Rob Scott

Aurum

This revised edition reprinted in 2010 by Aurum Press Limited,
7 Greenland Street, London NW1 0ND
www.aurumpress.co.uk

A catalogue record for this book is available from the British Library.

ISBN 978 1 84513 569 0
1 3 5 4 2
2010 2012 2013 2011

Book design by Robert Updegraff
Printed and bound in Italy by Printers Srl Trento

Title page: Rannoch Moor
Front cover: The Three Sisters of Glencoe from Stob Mhic Mhartuin

Aurum Press want to ensure that these National Trail Guides are always as
up to date as possible – but stiles collapse, pubs close and bus services
change all the time. If, on walking this path, you discover any important
changes of which future walkers need to be aware, do let us know. Either
email us on **trailguides@aurumpress.co.uk** with your comments, or if
you take the trouble to drop us a line to:
Trail Guides, Aurum Press, 7 Greenland Street, London NW1 0ND,
we'll send you a free guide of your choice as thanks.

CONTENTS

HOW TO USE THIS GUIDE

This guide is in three parts:
• The introduction, historical background to the area and advice for walkers.
• The path itself, described in seven chapters, with maps opposite each route description. This part of the guide also includes information on places of interest as well as descriptions of the routes to the summits of Ben Lomond and Ben Nevis, both of which lie just off the route of the West Highland Way. Key sites are numbered in the text and on the maps to make it easy to follow the route description.
• The last part includes useful information such as local transport, accommodation, organisations involved with the path, and further reading.

The maps have been prepared by Ordnance Survey for this guide using 1:25 000 Pathfinder maps as a base. In Scotland rights of way are not marked on Ordnance Survey maps, as is the case south of the border. The only established rights of way are those where a court case has resulted in a legal judgement, but there are thousands of other 'claimed' rights of way. Many paths and tracks were built by estates as stalking paths or for private access, therefore a path on a map is no indication of a right of way. While using such paths you should follow the Country Code, taking due care to avoid damage to property and the natural environment. The line of the West Highland Way is shown in yellow. Any parts of the path that may be difficult to follow on the ground are clearly highlighted in the route description, and important points to watch out for are marked with letters in each chapter, both in the text and on the maps. *Some maps start on a right-hand page and continue on the left-hand page - black arrows (→) at the edge of the maps indicate the start point.* Should there have been a need to alter the route since publication of this guide for any reason, walkers are advised to follow the waymarks or signs which have been put on the site to indicate this.

DISTANCE CHECKLIST

This list will help you in calculating the distances between places on the West Highland Way, whether you are planning overnight stops, lunch stops or checking your progress. Note that these are distances between points on the Way itself and do not include diversions to hotels, villages and so forth close to the route.

Location	Approximate distance from previous location	
	miles	km
Milngavie	0	0
Carbeth	4.5	7
Drymen	7.75	12.5
Balmaha	7	11
Rowardennan	6.5	10.5
Inversnaid	7	11.5
Inverarnan	6.25	10
Tyndrum	12	19
Bridge of Orchy	6.25	10
Inveroran	2.75	4.5
Kingshouse	9.5	15
Kinlochleven	9	14.5
Nevis Bridge, Fort William	14.25	23

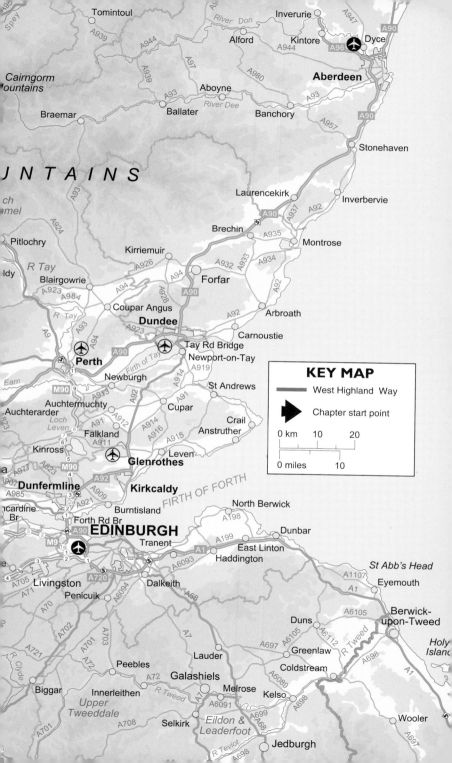

KEY MAP

West Highland Way

Chapter start point

0 km   10   20

0 miles   10

INTRODUCTION

WALKING THE WEST HIGHLAND WAY

The name suggests a walk where the dominant theme will be the grandeur of mountain scenery, and it does not disappoint. It begins quietly at the edge of Glasgow and builds up in a steady crescendo that ends with the arrival at the foot of Britain's highest mountain, Ben Nevis. But although the mountains provide the main theme, there are many variations to enjoy along the way.

The first part of the Way is very much Lowland in character, offering easy walking across farmland against a background of gentle hills, with higher peaks only appearing in the longer prospects. This section ends with the arrival at Loch Lomond and the start of the long walk up the eastern shore. The hills seem to fall almost sheer to the water's edge, their slopes densely covered in oak woods. Here the path must find its way as best it can, keeping mainly close to the loch shore. The result is a walk of great character, which combines the delights of mature woodland with its abundant and varied wildlife and the open vistas across the loch to the opposite shore and the mountains beyond. There is also, it has to be admitted, a certain piquancy in being able to glimpse frustrated motorists fuming in holiday traffic jams on the distant roads while one is enjoying the freedom and clean air of the walk.

Once Loch Lomond has been left behind, the character of the Way changes once again. The hills begin to crowd in, but the walking is generally comfortable, keeping to good tracks at the bottom of the glen. After the woodland, there is an openness everywhere and a real sense of being deep in true Highland country. Yet the presence of a modern road and railway means that at the same time the walker is always conscious of the contemporary world not too far away. All that changes at Bridge of Orchy and the crossing of Rannoch Moor. Here is a true wilderness, an inhospitable landscape of rough hummocks rising above dark, brackish pools. It ends in spectacular fashion with the arrival at Glencoe, and if anywhere can be said to epitomise the very best of Highland scenery then this is the place. The walk runs right past Buachaille Etive Mór, which is to the Highlands what the Matterhorn is to the Alps: a dramatic, challenging and most extraordinarily beautiful peak. It is here that the walk reaches its great climax in the climb up the Devil's Staircase to a summit from which a grand panorama of the Grampians can be enjoyed. This is followed by the descent to Loch Leven and another climb up to a second superb summit viewpoint before the walk gradually makes its way down to sea-level at Fort William.

The West Highland Way was the first official long-distance path to be established under the Countryside (Scotland) Act of 1967, and was officially opened in 1980. It was based on a number of far

Fine mountain scenery is a feature of the West Highland Way. This is a view of Glen Falloch near Inverarnan.

older routes: drove roads, military roads and, coming more up to date, abandoned railways. So, apart from offering heroic scenery, it is also a route deeply imbued with a sense of the past. The drove roads serve as reminders of the days when Highland cattle were regularly herded over long distances to the richer lands – and richer markets – of the Lowlands and northern England. There was another trade in cattle that went on at the same time, that of the reivers who came out of the glens to steal the cattle from the pastures. This was something more than a simple matter of lawlessness, it was a symptom of much deeper antagonisms, between Lowlander and Highlander, Catholic and Protestant, clan and clan. From this history came the romantic legends such as those of Rob Roy and the darker history of Glencoe and the Highland Clearances. One inescapable feature of the walk is abandoned farms, or even whole deserted villages, sad testaments to Highland depopulation.

The antagonisms reached their zenith in the Jacobite Rebellions, which brought the redcoats to the Highlands and set in train the long period of road-building by the military. But by the end of the eighteenth century there was a new interest in the Highlands. Travellers had discovered the delights of picturesque scenery, and nothing was more picturesque than the lochs and the heather-covered uplands of Scotland. The English still remained nervous about their northern neighbours. When James Boswell finally persuaded Dr Johnson to join him on a tour of his native land, the young Scot seemed less charitable than the visiting Englishman. They found themselves surrounded by curious Highlanders.

I observed to Dr. Johnson, it was much the same as being with a tribe of Indians. – JOHNSON. 'Yes, sir: but not so terrifying.'

But Scotland soon became popular, helped by the romances of Sir Walter Scott. By the second half of the nineteenth century it was all the rage, and had been given the royal seal of approval by Queen Victoria. This was the age of the vast sporting estates – of huntin', shootin' and fishin'. The railways helped to open up the region, and now tourists come here from around the world. There are still, however, vast areas which can only be reached by those who are prepared to make the effort of getting there on their own two feet, and the West Highland Way offers a chance to enjoy just such areas. There is a special satisfaction in taking in a superb view when one knows that one has earned the right to enjoy it, by one's own efforts – and that it can only be shared by others who come the same, hard route.

A Highland cow and her calf appear to be taking a rather glum view of passing walkers in Glencoe.

One of the gentler sections of the Way runs along the valley of the River Fillan.

There is also a special appeal in doing a long-distance walk as opposed to a series of shorter walks in an area. It provides a sense of continuity. One can feel and see the gradual changes in the landscape. Hints of change may be no more than the appearance of different-coloured stone beside the path, but they are hints that greater changes will soon be coming. The first, glorious sight of the mountains is all the more exciting when the day has begun among suburban houses.

This is a long-distance walk that is full of delights, a strenuous, but never over-demanding hill walk. It is, however, something more than a stroll through the country. One factor that bothers some, especially those not used to long walks, is the need to carry a back-pack. Most find it to be not so bad in practice as it may seem in contemplation, but for those who really cannot cope, there are carriers along much of the Way who will move your rucksack for you from stopping place to stopping place. But for everyone who sets off to walk the Way, it is as well to know what to expect and how best to cope with any likely problems. Notes for walkers tend, inevitably, to stress what can go wrong, which can be a little off-putting. They are not meant to be: knowing the potential problems in advance makes it less likely that you will encounter them, and if you do you should be suitably prepared.

By far the most important point is to be aware of the enormous difference the seasons make to this walk. Rannoch Moor in winter can be the most desolate place in Britain, and the path over the hills of Glencoe can be treacherous when rocks are covered in snow and ice. It is absolutely essential that walkers are aware of the need for proper mountain clothing and equipment for serious winter hill walking if they are not to endanger themselves and others who may have to rescue them. A winter walk can be splendid, but the description given here describes a walk taken when the snow is off the Way.

If the middle of winter is best left to the experienced, summer also has its disadvantages. It is not merely that more people come out to enjoy the sunshine: the insect population enjoys it just as much. It is difficult to decide which is the more unpleasant, the vicious clegs of early summer or the swarms of midges encountered later in the year. Early and late – May or June and September or October – will often provide the very best of conditions. There is one week that walkers might well wish to avoid. Each year a section of the Way between Bridge of Orchy and Fort William is used for the annual Scottish Motorcycle Trials. Timing varies from year to year, so it will be necessary to check with the Countryside Ranger Service (address at back of book). But whatever month is chosen, it is sensible to prepare for bad weather. The prevailing westerlies come with moisture-laden air that is lifted by the mountains to form rain clouds: it is possible to spend a week in Glencoe and never once see a summit; and while walking the Way in mid-May to prepare the notes for this book the author encountered everything from hot sunshine to snow squalls. All walks are more enjoyable if one is comfortable, warm and dry. That means proper walking boots, and genuinely waterproof clothing. Those who wear shorts should have a good insect repellent to ward off the ticks that lurk in the bracken.

Advance planning helps to ensure an enjoyable trip. Those who plan to camp *en route* will have more flexibility than those who have to look for overnight accommodation. The latter is sparsely spread along the route, and in the popular holiday periods it will almost certainly be necessary to book at least some nights in advance. This means that you should have a good idea of how far

Waterfalls are very much a feature of the mountain streams and rivers. These par

...n be seen near Tyndrum.

you can easily walk in a day. There are no rules for this, but many walkers find a week a comfortable time for the Way, which means averaging 13 miles (21 km) a day. On the whole the going is good, and the most difficult section is, perhaps surprisingly, not the Devil's Staircase, but the climb up from Kinlochleven. Many experienced walkers have been caught unawares by this section. The awkwardness of the terrain, where narrow paths are crossed by gnarled roots and are forced to wind their way through rocks and boulders, means that it is rarely possible to get into one's stride and walking pace is usually a good deal slower than one might expect. It is well worth looking at the map and reading the route description at the planning stage, so as to have an idea of where the difficulties are likely to crop up.

Following the route is not difficult as the Way is clearly marked with the symbol of a thistle set in a hexagon. Yellow arrows indicate where there is a change in direction, but walkers should be aware that waymarking itself is not sufficient to ensure that you get from one end of the walk to the other. The maps in this guide give you all the help you need in covering the route, but it is useful to carry either OS Landranger or Outdoor Leisure maps to give the wider picture. But maps are of little use without a compass, and a compass is only partially useful if you do not know how to use it to take bearings. Map and compass are absolutely essential for those who want to explore the countryside off the line of the Way. In the two months from mid-August to mid-October, however, it is essential that you get permission to leave established footpaths. This is deer-stalking season when the red deer are culled. You will be quite safe, however, walking on land owned by the National Trust for Scotland, where access is allowed throughout the year.

Finally, a word about safety. Accidents do happen and even something as minor as a sprained ankle can leave the walker stranded miles from help. Solitary walkers should always make sure that someone knows their route and where they are expecting to be at the end of the day. A torch is invaluable not just for finding the way after dark but as a signal to rescuers, and a whistle with a good loud blast is ideal for attracting attention. A simple first-aid kit should always be carried, and summer walkers would be advised to use insect repellent. In case this fails, some form of soothing cream for bites will make life a lot more pleasant.

The vast majority of walkers have no problems on the Way and simply enjoy an exhilarating walk through some of Britain's finest scenery.

Placid water, blue skies and hills combine to create an idyllic scene at the northern end of Loch Lomond.

Two contrasting environments: the blanket bog of Rannoch Moor with its peaty pools, and, beyond, the snow-capped Glencoe mountains.

GEOLOGY AND SCENERY

The diversity of scenery found along the Way has its origins in the underlying rocks, formed over vast, almost unimaginable periods of time. The walk begins in the Clyde valley, at the base of which lies the Old Red Sandstone laid down millions of years before man first appeared on the planet. These ancient rocks were not allowed to rest in peace. Volcanoes erupted through the crust, throwing up lava which flowed out over the land, building up in layer upon layer to form the Campsie Fells and the Kilpatrick Hills. Looking at the southern flanks of the Campsies you can still see how they were built up in tiers made up of no fewer than thirty separate flows of lava. Into this land a long glacial finger was pushed in the Ice Age, digging a trough that eventually filled with water to become Loch Lomond, and here, too, is one of the decisive scenic breaks of the Scottish landscape.

Standing on Conic Hill, you can see a ridge extending away to the east, while to the west a series of islands lines up like a flotilla in formation. This is the Highland Boundary Fault where in the imperceptibly slow movements of the earth's tectonic plates, the tough rock of the Highlands has met and ridden over the softer rocks of the valley. It was here that the glacier, forcing a difficult path through the harder rocks, now fanned out to create the shallower lake with its many small islands. To the north of the fault, as though to emphasise the change, Ben Lomond, the first true Highland mountain and the most southerly of the Munros – with peaks over 3000 feet (924 metres) – rears up. The granite hills of the Highlands are now never far away, mostly standing above valleys carved out by glaciers. Granites themselves are crystalline rocks, which typically sparkle in the sun, formed out of molten material forced up from the earth's core.

One of the great contrasts of the Way is the walk across Rannoch Moor to the mountains of Glencoe. The Moor itself is a blanket bog, a particular type of bog formed when heavy rainfalls combine with high humidity to keep an area saturated with water, rotting down plants to form acid peat. It is a curious, desolate area with its own vegetation, including one rush, *Scheuchzaria palustris*, unique to the area, and dotted with the whitened stumps of old pine trees.

The tall cliffs and rocky peaks that surround Glencoe were again formed when molten magma was forced up through faults

One of the most famous sections of the Way. The Devil's Staircase begins to twist and turn as it climbs out of Glencoe.

in the earth's surface. It is difficult to conceive what the earth must have been like in those far distant times, but something of the wild nature of the convulsions can still be sensed in the chaotic pattern of rocks reached above the Devil's Staircase. The greatest upheaval of all appears at the very end of the Way, with the mass of solidified lavas and volcanic rocks which form the smooth dome of Ben Nevis.

WILDLIFE

No one walking the Way is likely to remain unaware of the smaller representatives of the animal kingdom. Butterflies are common in the woods of Loch Lomond, and beetles can often be seen scurrying across the path. Unfortunately, the insect world even more often makes itself known in the irritating form of ticks, flies and midges. By way of compensation, there is the possibility of seeing some of the most magnificent animals and birds that the British Isles can boast.

The red deer richly deserves its popular title of 'Monarch of the Glen', and one would be very unfortunate if one failed to see one of these magnificent animals. But even if not visible they can often be heard, especially in autumn when the hoarse bellow of the stags echoes around crags and corries. The more elusive fallow deer may be spotted in wooded areas such as those on the banks of Loch Lomond, which are also home to wild goats. There is an interesting legend concerning these animals. Rob Roy is not the only famous name associated with caves along the way. It is said that Robert the Bruce, in his years on the run from the British, hid in a cave with his followers. It turned out also to be sheltering a small herd of goats who were shooed out. The pursuers, seeing the unconcerned, munching goats, assumed that there could be no one around and carried straight on. A grateful king later decreed that the wild goats should thereafter be for ever free to roam the woods undisturbed. For English visitors, one of the most attractive woodland residents is the red squirrel, now sadly almost extinct in mainland England. Other species are more difficult to spot; the pine marten is comparatively rare, while the wildcat, which makes its home among the crags and screes, is nocturnal. The hare does its best to avoid detection by changing to a white coat for winter camouflage against the snow. Voles, field mice and shrews can be seen, as well as their predators, stoats and weasels, which have been joined in recent years in Glencoe by mink, escapees from a local mink farm. Foxes are by no means uncommon, and there is a fair chance of seeing otters in the river valleys.

The bird-life of the area is no less spectacular. The golden eagle can be seen at the northern, more mountainous end of the Way. Smaller birds of prey include sparrow-hawk, kestrel, merlin, peregrine falcon and buzzard. The latter can be mistaken for the golden eagle – until one sees the great bird itself, then any doubt as to which is which is instantly removed. To see a pair of eagles out hunting is unforgettable, as they seem effortlessly to cover enormous distances, and ride the thermals with greater ease than any glider. At the opposite end of the scale are the birds more likely to be seen on the ground than in the air. Those who get up very early in the morning may see male black grouse strutting and displaying a fan of white tail-feathers to the generally bored-looking females. This usually takes place at a site, called a 'lek', on the edge of woodland, and it is in the woods that one may also catch a glimpse of Scotland's largest game bird, the capercaillie. This was shot to extinction in the 1780s but reintroduced from Sweden half a century later. Another secretive game bird is the ptarmigan, which makes its home on high moorland and mountain and, like the hare, takes on a protective white for winter. Other birds that

Colour and interest may be found anywhere. This rich and varied collection of mosses was spotted in a tiny stream near Ben Nevis.

are found in this area, but rarely further south, include the raven and the hooded crow. The woodland areas seem to constantly echo with bird song from the commoner species such as chaffinch and robin, and with the occasional, rarer call of the wood warbler, its single note accelerating to a melodious trill. In spring the cuckoo adds its own sarcastic comments on the walker struggling at the end of a long day under a heavy back-pack. As well as the more familiar water birds, there is also a chance of seeing either the red-throated or black-throated divers on the more remote lochs, particularly on the edge of Rannoch Moor.

With such a rich variety of wildlife, the slight extra effort of carrying a pair of binoculars on the walk should be amply repaid.

ROB ROY MACGREGOR

There are two Rob Roys: the romantic fictional hero of Sir Walter Scott and the actual man, who spent much of his life as an outlaw. The MacGregors were as quarrelsome as any of the Highland clans and, like the MacDonalds of Glencoe, they fell foul of the expansionist policy of the Campbells. Where the Highlanders were accustomed to settling such affairs with sword in hand, the Campbells were adept at using the law. The MacGregors were also famous 'reivers', raiding the Lowlands and the north of England for cattle. This was the society into which Rob Roy was born in 1671.

In his early years he was himself a notable reiver and a man of some importance: as tutor to his young nephew, the nominal chief of the MacGregors of Glen Gyle, he effectively held real power. He ran his own business as cattle drover and dealer, but in 1711 his head drover absconded with all the cash for the main cattle sales, leaving MacGregor in debt. The Duke of Montrose, a former friend and ally, now turned against him, demanding payment of money owed. When that was not forthcoming, he had him first bankrupted, then outlawed. His wife and family were turned out of their home near Inversnaid at the northern end of Loch Lomond and the home was burned. Rob Roy swore vengeance against Montrose, stealing his cattle and, it was said, kidnapping his men and holding them for ransom in either Rob Roy's Prison or Rob Roy's Cave, both of which are passed on the West Highland Way. He gained a reputation as the Robin Hood of Scotland. A typical tale recounts an event in 1716 when he heard of a widow who, like his own wife, faced eviction for debt by Montrose. He

The grandeur of the mountains. This is a view looking north across Glencoe, wit

is in the distance to the left.

called to see her and gave her the rent money, telling her to make sure she had a receipt. When the factor called, the debt was settled and the receipt duly handed over. On his way home he was stopped by Rob Roy and robbed: so in the best outlaw tradition, the widow's house was saved, the good outlaw got his money back again, and the wicked lord was discomfited. Rob Roy and the

The wild country of mountain and river to the north of Loch Lomond where the outlaw Rob Roy roamed.

MacGregors as a whole, however, were considered sufficiently troublesome for a garrison to be built at Inversnaid in 1718-19, which was the subject of another good story. Skilled masons and quarrymen were set to work preparing stone for the fortress, but in August 1718 they were rounded up by the MacGregors, carried away south to the Lowlands and sent on their way.

The Rob Roy stories have no doubt been elaborated and embroidered over the years. To some he was a partisan fighting for the rights of Highlanders against the devious machinations of rich Lowlanders. To others he was simply one more in a long line of reivers who plagued law-abiding neighbours. He was certainly not quite the daring man of legend, living wild with a price on his head, for he died peacefully in his own bed in his own house at Balquidder on the shores of Loch Voil at the respectable age of 63.

MILITARY ROADS

A good deal of the route of the Way follows the track of an old military road. The 1715 uprising revealed very quickly that the English troops were hampered by the absence of good roads for marching, while their opponents were moving over a terrain to which they had long been accustomed. In 1724 General Wade was sent to report on the situation, and he concluded that without a new road system the area could never be pacified. There followed many years of road construction, and one major link was the route from the Lowlands to Fort William. The southern section took the line used by the present road along the west bank of Loch Lomond, after which it turned east up Glen Falloch, and from there onwards military road and footpath are never far apart.

Often it is difficult to see the path as being anything other than a footpath, but there are still places where the nature of the original road is quite clearly revealed. At the beginning of the walk out of Tyndrum, for example, the cobbled surface remains intact, built like all the roads to a standard width of six feet, with drainage ditches to either side. A little further along, a typical rough, rounded arch bridge crosses the river, a utilitarian structure with no concessions to elegance. The most interesting section of the route is probably that between Bridge of Orchy and Kinlochleven, constructed after the 1745 rebellion, under the direction of Major William Caulfield. The bridge is again sturdy, but built on much finer lines than the one at Tyndrum. The next section is typical of the planning of the road system. Having kept comfortably to the

The clear mountain stream brings out the brilliance of stones, near the end of the Way on the approach to Glen Nevis.

floor of the glen for as far as possible, the engineers were now faced with the daunting prospect of Loch Tulla and the peat bogs of Rannoch Moor. They took what seemed the simplest way out, the one involving least engineering works, by hopping over the hill at the head of the loch instead of building causeways across the more marshy land at the foot. Zig-zagging up one side and down the other was the standard technique for all hill crossings. Between the Inveroran Hotel and Glencoe long stretches of sur-faced road have survived just to the north of the West Highland Way. The military road rejoins the footpath at Black Mount and here one can see how streamlets have been culverted under the road and larger streams crossed on flat-topped bridges. Hummocks beside the route have been broken into to provide stone for surfacing.

The next, and most spectacular, site of interest appears where the engineers were faced with the problem of getting out of Glencoe. The obvious answer would seem to be the one adopted by the road builders who followed on in 1785: go straight up the pass and then follow the coast northwards. But that involved the use of a ferry across Loch Leven near Ballachulish, not ideal for military uses. So once again the engineers decided to meet the challenge of the hills head-on, and built a zig-zagging road up the steep slope. It is said that the route was first given the name of 'The Devil's Staircase' by the soldiers who had the job of building it. Once over the summit the going was easier, but still involved hacking a way through the rocky landscape to allow carts, and even cannon, to use the route.

The web of roads that was thrown across the Highlands in the eighteenth century has been compared to the road system built up in Britain by the Romans. The similarity even led to a certain confusion further south. When an old surfaced track was uncov-ered across the North Yorkshire moor it seemed so similar to the Scottish military roads that it was named 'Wade's Causeway'. It was, in fact, a genuine Roman road. General Wade himself was among the first to point up the analogy. His finest bridge, across the Tay at Aberfeldy, carries just that message on commemorative plaques: once in English and then, to reinforce the point, again in Latin. In fact, the Romans generally worked faster, used better sur-veying techniques, and were more careful about such important matters as drainage than their successors. Nevertheless, the mili-tary roads were noteworthy achievements, which walkers on the West Highland Way have ample time to admire.

A dram at the end of the day has cheered many a walker: whisky barrels outside the Glengoyne distillery.

THE MASSACRE OF GLENCOE

Anyone visiting the region on one of those days when low clouds form a dark ceiling that stretches across the glen from hillside to hillside almost invariably thinks, if only for a moment, of the infamous massacre. It is an event that cannot be understood in isolation, but only as the culmination of years of feuding and bloodshed which arose out of the contrast between the more fertile, richer Lowland areas and the impoverished, remote Highlands. The inhabitants of the former were forever trying to extend their influence and landholdings, often with official government approval, while the Highlanders sought to redress the balance by cattle rustling. The Macdonalds of Glencoe were particularly adept at acquiring Campbell beef, but when they were caught, retribution was fierce: in one such encounter, 36 Macdonalds were caught and hung outside Mad Colin Campbell's castle. The final disaster to overtake the Macdonalds was due to their decision to back the wrong, that is the losing, side in the Civil War of the 1640s and they compounded their error, as far as the English establishment was concerned, by joining 'Bonnie Dundee' in fighting for the Stuart cause against William of Orange. The Campbells were constantly to be found in the opposing ranks.

The Jacobite resistance was broken at the Battle of Killiecrankie in 1689 and the defeated Highland chieftains were given until 1 January 1690 to swear the oath of allegiance to William III. A few, including the elderly Macdonald of Glencoe, put it off until the last moment. Held up in the end by bad weather he arrived at Fort William, only to be told that he had to travel on again to Inverary. There, a bitter pill, the oath was administered by Sir Colin Campbell. It was now five days after the deadline, yet that seemed to be the end of the affair. But the Macdonalds had made too many enemies, including the king, his Secretary of State, Sir John Dalrymple, and John Campbell, Earl of Breadalbane. The order went out that the Macdonalds were to be slaughtered: the government, the order declared, did not wish to be 'troubled with prisoners'. Now the treachery began that was to blacken the name of Glencoe.

On 1 February 1690, Captain Robert Campbell, a dissolute gambler and drunk, arrived in Glencoe with a troop of soldiers asking for billets. No one was suspicious; the oath had been given, and the officer, though a Campbell, had family connections with the Macdonalds. And there was one seemingly inviolate rule among the clans: they might murder each other, steal from each other, quarrel for centuries, but no one would ever abuse hospitality. The rule was about to be broken. On 12 February, Campbell received his orders to kill every Macdonald under the age of 70, and to take special care that the chief and his family, 'the old fox, nor none of his cubbs may get away'. Old tales have it that a fire was lit on Signal Rock at the western end of Glencoe to start the killings. How many of the soldiers spread out through the length of the glen saw the sign was uncertain, but in any event they killed slightly fewer than 40 people, and some 300 escaped, including two of the 'cubbs'. They took to the hills where cold, fatigue and starvation proved more efficient executioners. A second party of soldiers came over the pass to the north, now used by the West Highland Way, but arrived too late for the slaughter. It was not the end of the Macdonalds. They turned out to fight for the Stuart cause in 1715 and again in 1745, but the clan was finally broken at Culloden.

Bridge of Orchy, the last stage before the West Highland Railway heads off across the wastes of Rannoch Moor.

THE WEST HIGHLAND RAILWAY

The line accompanies the walk for much of the route, and for many walkers also provides the ideal means for returning to Glasgow in comfort when the end of the West Highland Way has been reached. Railway engineers, however, can rarely take the direct line available to walkers. One glance at the narrow strip of level land bordering southern Loch Lomond must have been all that was needed to convince them that this was not an ideal place for a railway. So instead they took a wide swing round, going out along the Clyde and up Gare Loch and Loch Long to Tarbet. Long-distance path and railway then remain close companions as far as Bridge of Orchy, beyond which the uninviting mountains of Glencoe rear up, and the engineers set off on another detour, this time across the scarcely more inviting wastes of Rannoch Moor. The story of the first railway surveyors' excursion across the Moor a century ago is truly remarkable.

They set out for a 40-mile journey across the Moor from Glen Spean on 30 January 1889. The group consisted of Robert McAlpine the contractor, three engineers, a solicitor and two factors from local estates, one of whom, John Bett, was 60 years old. Two of them, feeling some concern about the rigours of a Highland winter carried umbrellas! Everything went wrong from the start. A boat and boatman were supposed to be waiting to take them up Loch Treig, but neither could be found for a long time, and when the boat did appear it leaked. Cold and miserable, they went to the hunting lodge where they were promised a hot meal and beds: they got a cold snack and thin blankets. Undeterred they set off next morning on an ominously gloomy day, with sleet already whipping in their faces, to walk the last 23 miles over the moor. Sir Robert Menzies sent out his gamekeeper to offer them shelter halfway, but they refused and marched stoically on. Bett collapsed with exhaustion and was left with two of the others and one of the umbrellas. The party then split up and wandered off as night began to fall. Bullock, one of the engineers, walked into a fence in the dark and knocked himself out, but he at least realised that a fence meant habitation and followed it to a shepherd's hut, where he raised a rescue party. McAlpine eventually got off the moor after walking all night. The main group were brought to safety hours before a blizzard struck.

The line was finally opened in 1894. Walkers who look up to see passengers being carried past them in comfort might like to remember how much reckless effort went into making that comfort possible.

The magnificence of Glencoe, as the setting sun colours the peaks. It was amor

se beautiful mountains that the infamous massacre occurred.

THE
WEST HIGHLAND WAY

1 MILNGAVIE TO DRYMEN

via Dumgoyne and Gartness   *12 miles (19 km)*

So many walkers arrive at the start of the West Highland Way by train that the station **1** has become a semi-official starting point. In order to reach the station, however, one vital piece of information is essential: when asking for a ticket for the first stage, the name of the town and its station is pronounced 'mull-guy', though no one seems to have come up with a rational explanation of why this should be so. Having overcome that difficulty the walk itself can begin. Leave the station and cross the main road by the underpass, and continue along Station Road and Douglas Street to the little town square, where a splendid granite obelisk, carved with the thistle-in-the-hexagon emblem, has been erected to mark the opening of Scotland's first official long-distance path **A**. It shares the square with a short but ornate clock tower and a war memorial, where the draped lady points off into the distance, but not in the direction of the West Highland Way. Instead one turns right to

The official start of the West Highland Way in the town square at the centre of Milngavie.

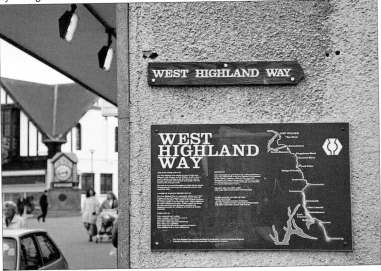

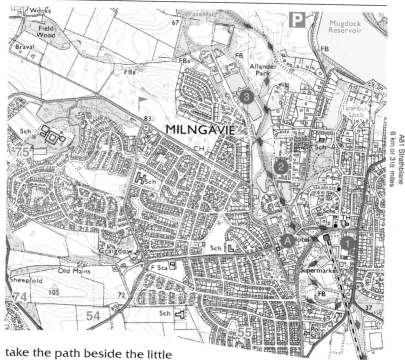

take the path beside the little
river, Allander Water. Cross over the road and
continue on the path following the course of the stream. As the
river bends away to the left, continue straight, on taking the path
under the road, which is actually the track bed of a railway serving
a former paper mill.

Now the buildings recede from view, and one could be walking
up a quiet country lane, overhung by trees. Where the path arrives
at a play area and a small pond **2** turn right to rejoin the riverbank.
This is still in the town, but the trees effectively filter out the sight
and sound of the traffic on the nearby roads. Then, as the town is
left behind, the countryside becomes much more dominant and a
good deal more attractive, with heavily scented pine and blazes
of rhododendron alongside the Way, until it opens out into an
area of rough scrub dotted with delicate silver birch. Beyond that
3 the path divides. Cross over a tiny stream and turn away from
the river to the right, going slightly uphill through an area of rough
moorland, brightened in season by patches of brilliant gorse. As
one climbs, so the view opens out and one has the first glimpse of
the surrounding hills, an attractive *hors d'oeuvre* for the main

Highland cattle are not the only local animals to boast splendid horns, as this ram proudly demonstrates.

course that is soon to follow. At the brow of the hill, the path swings round to the left and joins what was once the drive to Craigallian House. There is the same moorland and gorse, with a more open heather-covered hill to the right. All the time the path is becoming less of a route out of town and more of a pleasant country walk, and by the time it has run into the edge of Mugdock Wood **B,** urban landscapes are already forgotten. This is mixed woodland, dominated by birch, carpeted in spring with bluebells and wood anemones, and loud with birdsong and the hammering of woodpeckers. The river has now reappeared as a mountain stream, gurgling and splashing over a series of little falls, and the soggy land around it is speckled with marsh marigolds. There is also a new roughness in the land, as rocks push their way through the surface.

The driveway ends at a handsome Gothic lodge. Leave the wood by the gate **4**; turn left onto the road and almost immediately right through an ingenious type of stile that is a feature of this part of the walk. It is like the 'squeeze-stiles' familiar from many parts of Britain, except that the uprights are held in place by chains, so that they can easily be pushed apart and then fall back into place again. The path now follows a ledge above the river, the woodland ends and the view opens up to a hillside dotted with yellow gorse and patched with dark squares of conifers. It then descends to the river and a marshy area crossed by duckboards, with water iris to the side. A narrow, stony path then goes forward and runs into a wider track which winds down a little hollow between low hills.

As the walker rounds a corner of woodland **C** a splendid view opens up over Craigallian Loch, with the wooded hill of Dumgoyach up ahead. Buzzards are regular visitors, patrolling the air above the woods in a constant search for prey, but the loch appears to be a lonely home for a solitary moorhen. The imposing romantic mansion of Craigallian House stands to the south of the loch.

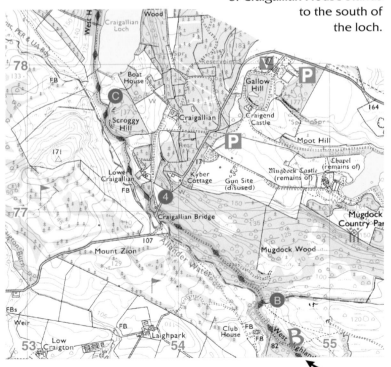

Then the view is temporarily lost as the path disappears into a conifer plantation. As the woodland ends the broad track swings round to the right past a selection of pleasantly ramshackle holiday chalets, which have a jolly, home-made air that owes very little to architectural theory. Carbeth Loch is smaller than Craigallian but has a good deal of quiet charm and, it seems, a larger and more enthusiastic bird population. The area immediately beyond it is green, quite lush grassland with a flock of well-fed sheep. The track now leads up to the road **5.** Turn left. There is now a good view over to the right of the Campsie Fells which, with their distinctive terraces, look from a distance like a vast, striped layer-cake. At the end of the range, Dumgoyach pops up again like a neat, fancy bun. At the white house turn right off the road through the stile **6**.

The character of the landscape now begins to change, as the track passes through farmland grazed by cattle, but an even bigger change lies just ahead. The path climbs up to a stone stile **D** and suddenly one feels that the Way is earning its title, for here is true Highland scenery. In the foreground are the Kilpatrick and Campsie Hills and through the gap in between there is a splendid panorama of the mountains that surround Loch Lomond, real mountains that for much of the year carry snow in hollows around their peaks. The path runs on through an area of rough moorland with hillocks and bracken, where the pure, high call of the curlew cuts through the mountain air. It leads downhill, swinging right away from the farm buildings, then

Young bullocks warily eyeing walkers at Carbeth.

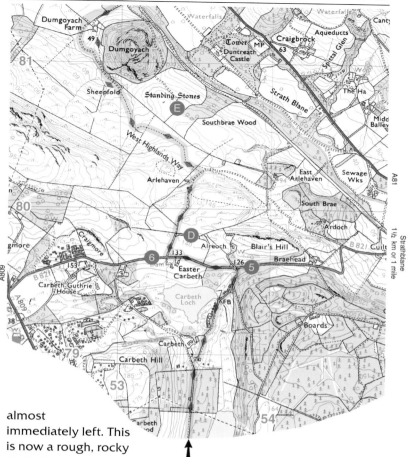

almost immediately left. This is now a rough, rocky track through an area of coarse tufts of spiky grass and peaty brown streams. Over to the right, beyond the squared-off lines of the conifer plantation is a short line of massive boulders, set in place in the New Stone Age, the Dumgoyach Standing Stones **E**. The path now passes round the foot of Dumgoyach Hill, so densely packed with trees that it looks rather like an old-fashioned plush pincushion. Getting closer, the walker sees crags lurking among the trees. The path then passes in front of a farmhouse with typical dormer windows. Cross over the wooden stile at the end of the stone wall, and now the landscape changes again. Instead of the rough moor there is flat grassland, grazed by sheep and cattle, with the occasional pheasant that has wandered out of the woods for a peck at the grain. Turn right on to the driveway that leads away

Shapely copper whisky stills, built to a design that has remained virtually unchanged since the last century.

from the farm to cross the wooden footbridge over Blane Water, and immediately beyond that a straight embankment can be seen crossing the fields, and it is not difficult to guess that one has arrived at an old railway line. This was the Blane Valley Railway, originally built in 1867 to link Killearn to lines running into Glasgow. It was extended to Aberfoyle then absorbed into the larger North British system, but nothing could prevent the little-used line from closure even before Dr Beeching wielded his famous axe. On reaching the embankment **7** turn left onto the former track bed, which provides easy walking for the next few miles, straight through the middle of the gap between the hills. As one passes through a small, dense conifer plantation it becomes clear that what appeared at first to be a conventional railway embankment is a flood-bank, protecting the line from the wet, marshy land along the river. Over to the right, a group of white buildings and a tall chimney come into view, including a building with a small pagoda roof, the sure sign of a whisky distillery. This is the Glengoyne distillery **F**, built in 1833 and taking its water from the falls behind the buildings. A footpath leads off from the Way for those who would like a visit and a guided tour.

The path now reaches an open area which marks the site of a former station **G** and walkers might feel inclined to do as the trains did, and stop for a while, for next to the line is what was once the village store, now converted into a pub. Inside are old photographs showing the area in its railway days. The path crosses the road and continues on following the old railway track, which runs through pasture

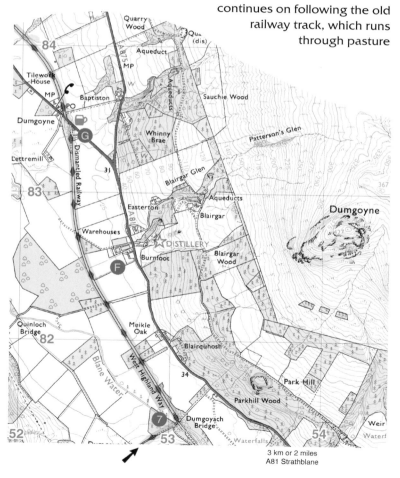

3 km or 2 miles
A81 Strathblane

where the grazing herds include a number of shaggy, long-horned Highland cattle. The line runs on a low embankment which has provided a home for a large colony of rabbits. Another minor road is crossed, and now the path is a good deal narrower and less obviously railway-like. It passes along the backs of houses and close by a main road. The noise of traffic is slightly deadened by a thin strip of woodland, and almost overpowered by the raucous cacophony from a rookery. The Way is temporarily diverted by a farm where the old railway bridge has been blocked in, but immediately continues back on the same line once the obstacle has been passed. The B834 crosses the line on an iron bridge carried on stone piers. Below it the ground becomes quite muddy, and would be a great deal worse where a farm track joins in if old wooden sleepers had not been laid down to provide a dry pathway. This is all very placid countryside with a gentle swell of neat, green fields, dotted with small woods. There is a shallow cutting, then another road is crossed and the last part of the railway section of the Way appears as a cindery path. At the next bridge **8** take the path that climbs up to the road and turn left.

The road runs down to the river, Endrick Water. To the right the water tumbles over a weir, above which a mill leat has been constructed. To the left it falls over a series of sandstone ledges, worn down into rounded, sculptural shapes. A row of cottages of the same

The falls beneath the road bridge at Gartness.

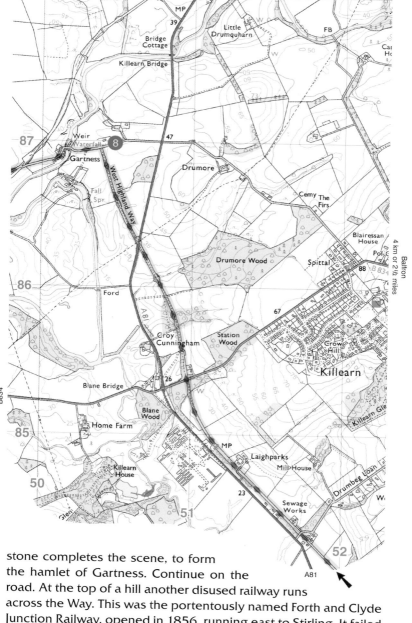

stone completes the scene, to form
the hamlet of Gartness. Continue on the
road. At the top of a hill another disused railway runs
across the Way. This was the portentously named Forth and Clyde
Junction Railway, opened in 1856, running east to Stirling. It failed
to live up to the grandeur of its title, closing down in 1934. From

The end of the long line of the Campsie Fells is marked by the rocky hump of Dumgo

Spring flowers soften the hard outline of the solid sandstone houses of the hamlet of Gartness.

here there is a lovely view down the placid river valley. Continue straight on at the crossroads at the top of the hill, and now the Way becomes noticeably hillier again. The old railway swings away, heading west, and the road runs along the rim of a delightful little valley where a stream meanders below a hillside splashed with gorse. Where the road divides continue straight on. A fine tree-lined drive leads away to Drumquhassle House, and beyond that is the site of a Roman fort, but there is no point looking for traces, for the outline can only be seen from the air and even then only as a faint shadow on the ground. From the top of the hill **H** there is a mixture of views. Over to the right the stepped outline of the Campsie Hills is easily seen; to the left there is a first, brief glimpse of Loch Lomond, while up ahead is a large, noisy quarry. The road runs along the edge of the quarry, then turns sharply left. Just before the small bridge over the stream **9** turn right onto the foot-path. Many walkers will want, however, to carry straight on down the road to Drymen with its shops, hotels, pubs and restaurant.

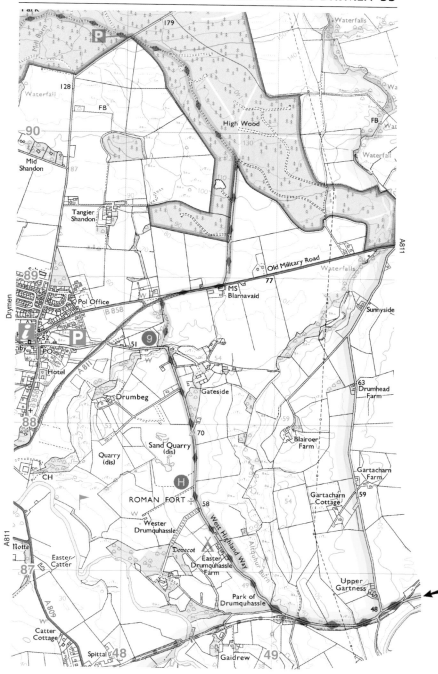

Rain clouds swoop low over the row of islands that marks the position of the Hig

as it crosses Loch Lomond.

Along the Way on the approach to Conic Hill.

2 DRYMEN TO ROWARDENNAN

via Balmaha   *13 miles (21 km)*

This section of the walk provides the first introduction to Loch Lomond, and a real sense of rough, tough walking in Highland scenery. Those who have gone into Drymen should now retrace their steps to the path by the bridge **9**. The Way now heads uphill towards the wooden post on the crest and across the field, past the woodland on the left. At the roadway **10** cross over and turn right to take the small path beside the road's edge. This is the A811, built on the alignment of the earlier military road. The eighteenth-century roads built by the army have often been compared to those of a much earlier generation of engineers, the men of the Roman legions, and this one, built after the 1745 rebellion, certainly has a true Roman straightness. Turn left at Blarnavaid Farm **11**, going through the stile to follow the path beside the fence leading up to the forest. The first part of the path passes along an avenue of gorse bushes, and then runs up alongside the woods. There is a last chance to enjoy a glance back at the panorama of the Campsie Fells before plunging into the woods. Almost immediately, turn left **12** onto the broad track. This is a densely packed plantation, established in the 1930s, with seemingly endless rows of mature trees retreating to the dark interior. Wildlife, however, is plentiful. Rabbits scurry across the track, and birdsong echoes among the trees. At the first path junction, follow the main broad track that swings round to the left through an increasingly glum woodland, in which mossy stumps provide the only colour. Emerging briefly from the trees, one catches a glimpse of Loch Lomond. At the roadway **13** turn left then immediately right onto the forest track. The path now has newly planted tress to one side, so there is a welcome sense of openness again and views of peaks beyond the forest. Unlike many forest paths, this one does have the advantage of being dry under foot, with a surface rather like a rough, cobbled street.

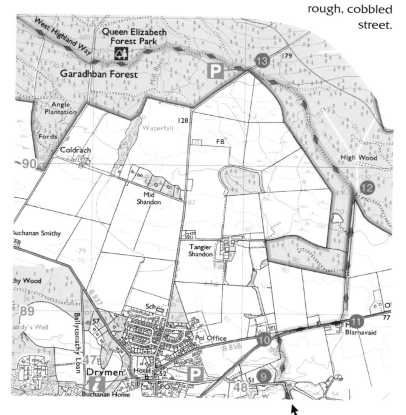

Many woodland birds are present, and even if you do not see a capercaillie you may hear one blundering around rather noisily among the trees. Small burns occasionally cross the route, gurgling through the rocks as they plunge down the hill. There are also welcome intrusions of Scots pines, survivors from a much older forest. Eventually the path emerges from the woods **14** by an area of felled trees with a view out over Loch Lomond.

There are now two alternative routes to Balmaha, though walkers may not be given the choice. During the lambing season, the more attractive route over Conic Hill is closed for about a month, between mid-April and mid-May. The alternative is simple to follow, and will be briefly described. It follows the obvious forest track down towards the road and offers tantalising views of Conic Hill itself which from here has the humpy shape of a dragon's back. It eventually becomes a surfaced road that joins the B837 at Milton of Buchanan. Turn right here past an old watermill beside the Burn of Mar and keep to the road as far as the large car park at Balmaha where the two routes are reunited.

The main track is a continuation from **14** following the same general direction as the previous section of forest track. It soon swings round to the right and begins to climb steadily uphill. The trees then close in again until the forest edge is reached **15**. Cross over the high stile on to the rough, bracken-covered moorland, an area where a grouse is quite likely to start up from cover with a noisy whirr of wings. Follow the edge of the dike up the hill to the right then round to the left to cross a busy burn on a footbridge. The path now leads on to the more impressive Burn of Mar **A** running through a little gorge shaded by birch and rowan. Dippers can usually be spotted hopping from rock to rock

in the stream below the bridge. The next part of the route is all too easy to follow: it simply heads straight up the ridge towards the summit of Conic Hill, the first significant climb of the walk, with a total rise of over 500 feet, or just under 200 metres. The Way goes on up through the heather to pass just below the summit on a convenient, natural ledge on the far side of the hill. It is well worth the effort, however, to climb the extra short distance to the top **B** to enjoy the view of the string of islands in Loch Lomond far below, and looking east on a clear day it is possible to pick out the exotic Gothic tower of the Wallace Monument, over 20 miles away.

The main track continues along the side of the hill, now going steadily downhill. Where the paths divide **16** turn left through the gap between the two humps then round to the right to continue on the far side of the ridge, winding round the gorse-covered, knobbly hill heading for the gate at the edge of the woods. Beyond the gate take the path heading downhill between the spruce and pine. At the junction of the tracks **17** turn right and continue downhill past a reedy pond. Leave the woods at the car park and head down to Balmaha and the road **18**.

Turn right at the road to the little bay at Balmaha, with its hotel looking out over a cluster of small boats. A path runs along the edge of the bay on duckboards and then continues round, hugging the loch shore. The shore road now reaches a dead-end. A few paces beyond that, turn right up the steps that mark the start of the steep path that climbs to the top of Craigie Fort **C**. This rocky knoll provides another splendid viewpoint, with the densely wooded, rocky island of Inchcailloch directly opposite, and the more elongated island of Inchfad next to it, boasting what must be the ideal house for anyone looking for privacy combined with spectacular scenery. It also provides the first hint of what the long walk up Loch Lomond will be like: no stroll by the water's edge, but a series of frequently steep climbs and descents on often very rough paths. For now, having arrived at the top of the knoll, the path promptly turns back down to the water's edge on the far side of the hill. The happy discovery is that the surroundings are no longer limited to conifers, for this is attractive deciduous woodland, dominated by oak. The woods

Pleasure boats lie at their moorings in the inlet that forms a safe haven at Balmaha.

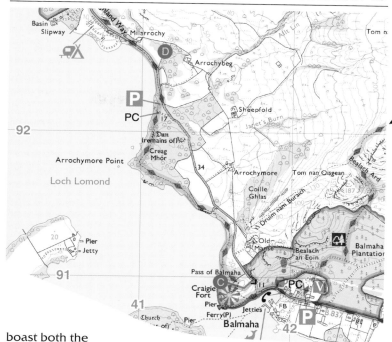

boast both the
pendunculate or English oak and
the sessile oak, together with a few hybrids in between. Once back
at the shoreline, the Way does offer a pleasant lochside saunter,
which is particularly attractive in spring when the woodland floor is
spattered with bluebells, snowdrops and primroses. The area is
well drained and where the water channels cross the path they are
contained in little natural stone conduits, an excellent example of
how a walk can be kept comfortable in an apparently natural,
unobtrusive way. The care shown in such details does a great deal to
maintain the essential character of the Way.

This is woodland full of variety and interest, where rocks push out
through the soil and trees fight to find room in between, curling and
twisting their roots round the stones like gnarled fingers clutching a
ball. The path keeps close to the shore round Arrochymore Point
then rejoins the road near a car park and picnic site **D**. This is a popular spot in summer for walkers to rest and for others to simply sit
back, enjoy the sun and watch the wind surfers and dinghy sailors
out on the loch. The route now has to go round the back of a large
caravan park, but has its own path a little separated from the road. It
crosses a small stream and enters woodland dominated by one

massive, ancient oak. The path crosses the road, but continues in the same direction through the edge of the Queen Elizabeth Forest Park. It is a quiet road so there is little to disturb the pleasures of the landscape of sparse woodland and heather-covered hills. The Way crosses a small stream and a house driveway **19** and then turns away up wooden steps. It curves briefly back towards the road then swings decisively away in the direction of the loch.

Until recently, this whole area was blanketed with conifers, which have now been felled and the ground replanted with oak. A clear path leads up to a gate in the tall deer fence and now there are magnificent views out over the loch to the hills on the far side, dominated by the anvil-shaped summit that gives The Cobbler its name. After following a very wandering route, the path delivers you out of the enclosure by a second gate and back onto the road from which you started this detour. Cross straight over the road to take the footpath which begins by the Welcome to Cashel sign, and turn left. This is a region which has been designated for replanting with native trees. After crossing the Cashell Burn, turn right by the caravan and camping site **20** onto the path that climbs a little way up the hill, parallels the road and after a few hundred yards drops down again. Continuing on the road one can feel grateful for being on this side of the loch, for across the water you can see

There is little space for the walker along the side of Loch Lomond.

the endless stream
of traffic on the opposite bank.

Immediately beyond Sallochy House **21** turn left into the woodland though clumps of rhododendrons. The path leads down to the
shore and, having got there, promptly turns away again to climb a
small hill. Having got to the top one can see why, for a crag falls
away sheer to the water's edge. There are fine views from the top
but now, like the Duke of York's men, you have to march back down
again. There is now a gentle, wavering meander through the trees,
where local bird-life has been encouraged by the provision of nest-
ing boxes.

There is another break in the trees by a road that provides access to a small car park and picnic area. Continue straight on along the side of the loch, cross the footbridge over the stream and follow the path at the water's edge. There is a little scramble over rocks streaked with quartz before a small inlet with jetty and boathouse is reached. Go round the back of the boathouse and climb up to a broad track that again takes to the shore. By a memorial seat at the end of the inlet **22** turn right off the broad track on to a steep, narrow, stony path that goes sharply uphill. The Way now heads into a gloomy conifer plantation, offering a brief respite before once again heading uphill, this time on a track criss-crossed by gnarled roots, polished by countless passing boots. At the top are the crumbling remains of a tower, after which the path begins squirming its way downhill again. Once more felling has opened up the view and a new path has been laid down, which is very easy to follow. It swings round to the right, to an area of coppiced woodland, and through the breaks in the trees Ben Lomond can be seen, dominating the whole area.

Eventually and inevitably, the path returns to the side of the loch by a little shingly beach **E** and an attractive stone house. Just off-shore is a *crannog*, an artificial island built up from rocks to support a small timber house or houses. The earliest date from the Bronze Age, but excavation has revealed Iron Age material as well. There are a number in the loch, mostly submerged and only visible during droughts. Cross the burn on the footbridge for another section of easy walking through mixed woodland. A rather grand wooden footbridge crosses the gently flowing Wood Burn. Beyond that is an old stone wall marking a forest boundary, followed by a somewhat wavering path through a lumpy, rocky landscape. Eventually it emerges beside the road with a fine view of the mountains that cluster at the end of the loch. Carry straight on past the roadside car park 23 at the head of a small inlet, to take the recently constructed path that leads away from the loch, round the back of a pine-studded knoll. Go past the interpretation centre which, at the time of writing, was still under construction, to take a route through a jumble of rocks, some way above the edge of the loch. Rowardennan comes briefly into view, but one more hump rears up before it can be reached. Rough stone steps lead up to the top of the hill with a crown of rhododendrons, and the path on the other side comes back to a small bay with boats and a cluster of chalets. The track turns inland to go round the chalet park. Turn left at the road to walk into Rowardennan **24**.

The bay and ferry pier at Rowardennan.

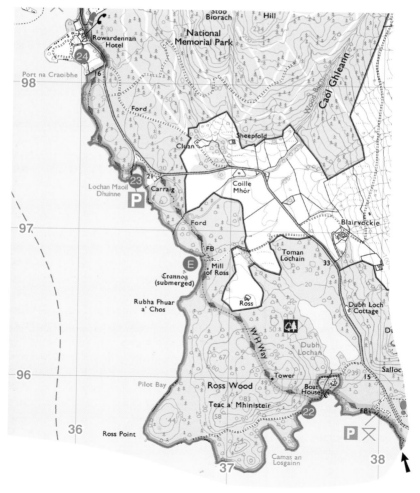

THE ASCENT OF BEN LOMOND

7½ miles (12km) return trip

Many walkers who stop at Rowardennan are tempted to take a half day away from the West Highland Way for an ascent of Ben Lomond. It is certainly very rewarding, but one has to bear in mind that this is an ascent to over 3000 feet (914 metres) and weather has to be taken into account. In winter, in particular, snow and ice will make the upper part of the climb a real and serious danger to all but those who are used to, and equipped for, the conditions. And even in summer, the whole summit can rapidly be covered by cloud and chilling rain. That being said, thousands happily make the ascent every year.

The route is easy to follow and starts opposite the Rowardennan Hotel on the path that curves steadily round to the right away down the road. After a short distance, a second path, which starts at the car park near the jetty, joins in from the left. The paths combine to go straight up the wide ride through a plantation of spruce and larch. It is a steady climb, broken by a bridge over a burn and a short flight of rough stone steps to help ease the way over a difficult section. The path emerges from the wood via a wooden gate to the rather daunting prospect of a very steep hillside up ahead. This is also a walk of 'false summits'; the nearer you get to what looks like being the top, the more hillside seems to appear in front of you. Fortunately, there are such good views back down over Loch Lomond that there is every excuse to stop for a breather.

Eventually the gradient begins to ease, and the path now heads up towards the summit ridge. After a steep climb it turns left below the rocks on an easy gradient to reach the summit itself at a height of 3194 feet (974 metres). Loch Lomond lies spread at your feet, with the mountains aptly known as the Arrochar Alps beyond at the head of Loch Long. You can look back to the Campsie Fells and the gap through which the West Highland Way passes. To the north-east beautiful Loch Katrine lies snugly in the heart of the Trossachs and one may even see the pleasure steamer *Sir Walter Scott* puffing serenely across its waters. The loch provides Glasgow with water, so steam is still used to prevent possible pollution by diesel or petrol. Away to the north are the Grampians that will be met later along the Way.

Having reached the summit and enjoyed the views, all that remains is to turn round and come back down again.

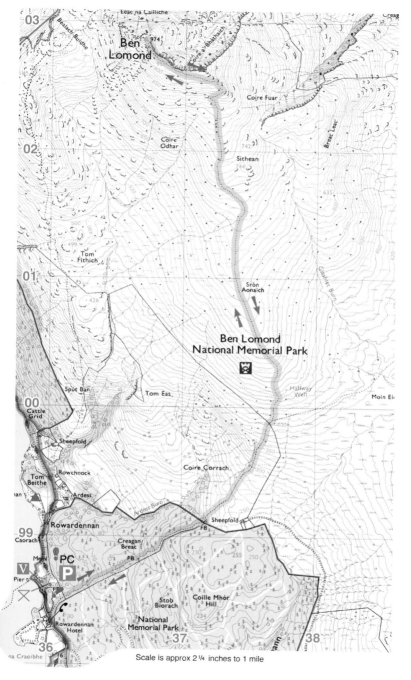

Scale is approx 2¼ inches to 1 mile

Ben Lomond: those who take the extra walk to the summit are rewarded by magn

3 ROWARDENNAN TO INVERARNAN

via Inversnaid   *13 miles (21 km)*

This final section up Loch Lomond has a somewhat fearsome reputation for being rough and difficult, but walkers will find that new path building has eased the way through the problem areas. Rowardennan itself is an attractive spot with a large hotel, a jetty where the ferry from Inverbeg calls in and a splendid panorama of mountains. The road continues around the bay then degenerates into a rougher track. Follow this round to the right at the entrance to the youth hostel **25** then almost immediately turn left where the path divides. This is an opportunity to warm up for what lies ahead, for it is a gentle stroll through oak woodland bursting with rhododendrons, and all set under the impressive bulk of Ben Lomond. The track soon returns to the lochside, as a tree-shaded way at the foot of a steep hillside. It eventually emerges by a small promontory, The Yett of Ptarmigan, with a cosy house enjoying a quite magnificent setting.

Ben Lomond, dusted by overnight snow, seen from Rowardennan.

The track has to make its way round the back of the promontory, passing the even grander Ptarmigan Lodge. Approximately 300 yards (300 metres) beyond this point **26** the Way divides, but it is easy to miss the junction. There is a high-level route which involves nothing more complicated than staying on the same forest track for the next 3 miles (5 km). The alternative, lower route, a narrow track that hugs the shore line, is closed at present as it has become dangerous. There are, however, plans to reopen it as soon as it can be made safe. Walkers should look for appropriate signs, or consult the Ranger Service, before attempting the lower route. Both routes will be described starting with the lower.

The route from **26** goes downhill on rough-hewn steps to the water's edge. It is wooded throughout, the dark oak and light birch providing a pleasant contrast. Tangled roots, shattered crags and boulders result in a certain amount of scrambling to find the easiest route. The path makes a temporary slight diversion inland to cut behind the headland of Rubha Curraichd, but otherwise seldom strays far from the loch. Approximately half a mile (1 km) from the headland, a particularly impressive crag rears up, known as Rob Roy's Prison **A**. The outlaw is said to have used a cave in the rocks to hold prisoners and hostages when he was active here in the early years of the eighteenth century. He would certainly have been little disturbed by passers-by, so the old oral tradition might well be true. Beyond the prison **27** a track leads down from the high-level route. Keep to the left on the path that goes uphill into an area of woodland now dominated by conifers. Just beyond the crest of the hill is Rowchoish bothy **B**. Tumbled stone walls are all that remain as reminders of the community that once lived in what was then a small hamlet. There are splendid views past Tarbet on the far shore down to the mountains above Arrochar on Loch Long. From here it is only a short uphill walk through the woods to join the upper route at **28**.

The upper route throughout stays on the forest track, which lies on a ledge carved from the hillside and generally keeping to the contours: in places one can see drill marks in the pathside crags indicating where the rock was split apart. When the branches are bare, there are views through the trees down to the loch, but the Way itself is not devoid of interest. Streams tumble down the hill and across the Way, and one in particular, by a horseshoe bend, dashes down through an eerie and romantically dark, rock-filled gully. In places the views are completely lost as the track passes through spruce, but there are always a few gaps where the view can be enjoyed. A grassy knoll **C** is provided with a bench seat and offers much the same view, but from a higher elevation, as Rowchoish bothy on the other path. It looks straight over to three-summited Ben Arthur, which owes its other name, The Cobbler, to the rocky peak shaped very like a shoemaker's last. Just past this point, the Way divides **29**, the route to the left leading down to the other path. The main route carries on to **28**.

Walkers who have followed the lower route may now feel a sense of relief at finding themselves on an easier track, but it is short-lived. Almost immediately the broad way peters out and continues straight on as a narrow footpath, meandering through

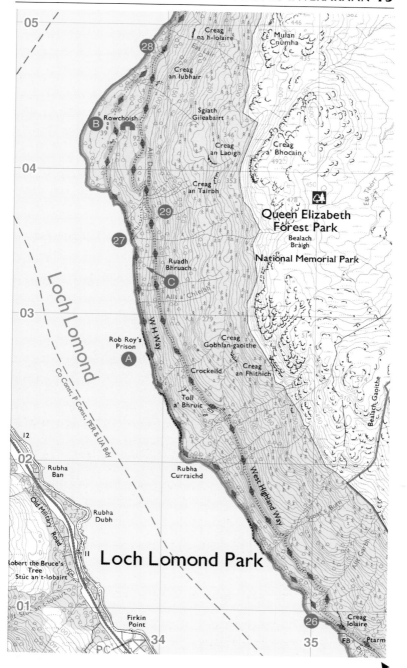

05

Creag
na h-Iolaire

28

Mulan
Cnumha

446

Creag
an Iubhair

Rowchoish
B
39

Sgiath
Gileabairt

Creag
a' Bhocain
492

346

Creag
an Laoigh

04

478

Creag
an Tairbh
353

450

Queen Elizabeth
Forest Park

29

Bealach
Bràigh

27

National Memorial Park

Ruadh
Bhruach

C

Allt a' Chalbh

03

279

W H Way

Rob Roy's
Prison
A

Creag
Gobhlan-gaoithe

574

Creag
an Fhithich

Crockeild

Toll
a' Bhruic

Loch Lomond

Co Const, P Const, PER & UA Bdy

12

West Highland Way

Bealach Gaoithe

02

Rubha
Ban

Rubha
Curraichd

Old Military Road

27

Rubha
Dubh

11

Robert the Bruce's
Tree
Stùc an t-Iobairt

Loch Lomond Park

01

26

Creag
Iolaire

Firkin
Point

FB

Ptarm

PC

34

35

The northern end of Loch Lomond, looking towards the peaks that rise up around Glen Falloch.

an area where a lot of tree cutting has taken place. This is, how-ever, the start of the new, improved pathway which begins with a stiff climb, then levels out to run round the side of the hill. The first of a number of mountain streams appears, tumbling down in a series of short, burbling falls and crossed on large boulders. This is a very attractive section, passing through broad-leaved woodland, where each opening in the trees seems to provide a better view than the last. After more falls, where the water streams down glistening slabs, there is a sharp descent to the lochside to arrive at a more open stretch of the walk, below a bracken-covered slope that climbs to a craggy summit. A footbridge crosses the Cailness Burn, where a house **D**, enjoys an idyllic setting.

The path leads on to a small bay and more panoramic views, before heading off to a very much rougher section of the Way. It begins with a climb, involving scrambling over rocks and gnarled roots, and is soon followed by an equally interesting descent, with a shuffle along a narrow stone ledge above the dark waters of the loch. The route continues to switchback between shore and hillside and it is in such areas that one is likely, forewarned by their distinctive musky smell, to encounter a herd of feral goats. In general, they show little interest in passing walkers. There are deer too in these woods, though one has to be quiet and patient to see them. Birdsong is a constant companion, with woodpeckers adding a percussion accompaniment. Many different species can be seen,

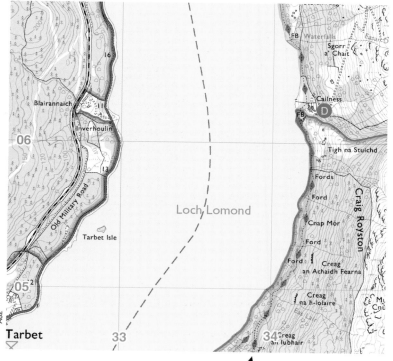

from sandpipers, dippers and wagtails at the shoreline to buzzards riding the air above the hills, giving out their distinctive mewing call. Finally the Inversnaid Hotel **E** comes into view. Cross the spectacular waterfalls on the footbridge to arrive at the hotel itself, the only spot offering refreshment along this part of the route.

The Way passes in front of the hotel and continues as a wide track by the lochside, with a view across to the hydro-electric station on the opposite bank. It comes out by a corrugated-iron boathouse. There is an RSPB trail for bird-watchers turning off at this point, for one is now in the Inversnaid Nature Reserve, but the main route goes straight on over the footbridge. The path soon narrows down, but the going remains easy, providing a pleasant walk with few disturbances apart from the occasional rattle of a train, usually invisible among the trees across the loch. But soon the path begins to climb and the way becomes steadily rougher until it is almost blocked by crags and boulders. It is possible to find a way by the water's edge, but it is slightly easier scrambling at the foot of the cliffs. It is up here that one will find another of Rob Roy's hide-outs, his cave **F**. It is not, to be honest, much of a cave, more a gloomy cleft which it is hard to imagine even a hard-pressed outlaw occupying for very long.

One of the few open sections of the lochside walk, at Doune.

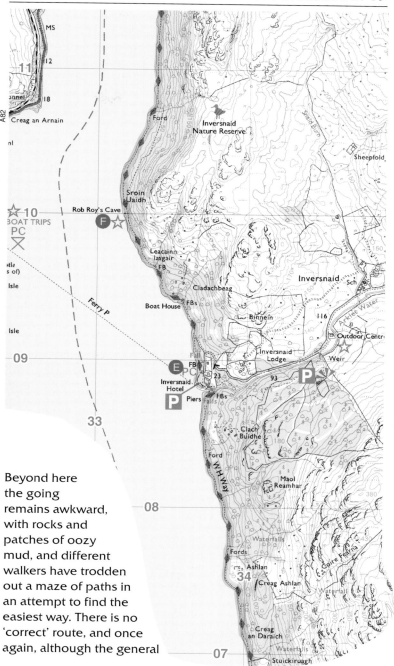

Beyond here the going remains awkward, with rocks and patches of oozy mud, and different walkers have trodden out a maze of paths in an attempt to find the easiest way. There is no 'correct' route, and once again, although the general direction is clear, the details have to be a matter of choice. After a while, the path once again becomes a more definite single way and the walking is altogether easier. This is a landscape where massive boulders dot the hillside and fill the gullies that carry the hill streams. Returning down to the shore there is a tight squeeze between a boulder and a tree, just about wide enough to take a walker and pack. The lochside path still has its ups and downs, but the going has eased. Up ahead the little island of I Vow **G** can be seen, a useful landmark roughly halfway between the Inversnaid Hotel and the point where the West Highland Way finally leaves Loch Lomond. There is, however, quite a lot of work still to be done, with a good many ups and downs and a damp reedy area, very popular with the dreaded midges. A footbridge marks the end of the Nature Reserve, and now the path rears up so steeply that a ladder has been provided, shortly followed by a bridge crossing a stream that trickles down over shiny black rock. This gives way to one of those by now quite familiar sections of labyrinthine ways over and round rocks, which ends at a little shingle beach. The loch has now narrowed considerably and the busy traffic on the far side seems noisily close.

Cross over a small footbridge **30**, and turn to the right on to the path across the grass, keeping the large, prominent rock to your right. Cross the bridge over the burn, and turn right onto the track that heads off down an attractive little wooded valley, with a stream winding and trickling down the middle. This represents a very definite change in the landscape, which is now divided up by walls of immense boulders. Sheep graze the rough grass, and the route seems, and almost is, open all the way to the distant hills. But there is to be one more return to the water, on a path like a roughly cobbled street, and now the whitewashed houses at the head of the loch come into view. But this time the land slopes gently away and the walking is altogether more comfortable. At a little bay the path begins to swing away, leaving the loch for the last time. It crosses a footbridge and then a stile **31** where there is access to the summer ferry that takes passengers across to Ardlui.

The sense that the nature of the walk is changing is now definitely confirmed. Instead of dense woodland, there is now grassland grazed by sheep. A short, steep climb leads to a point where the path contours the side of the hill. It crosses a wooden footbridge, then bends to the right and there is a chance to look back again at Loch Lomond, while up ahead the view is dominated by

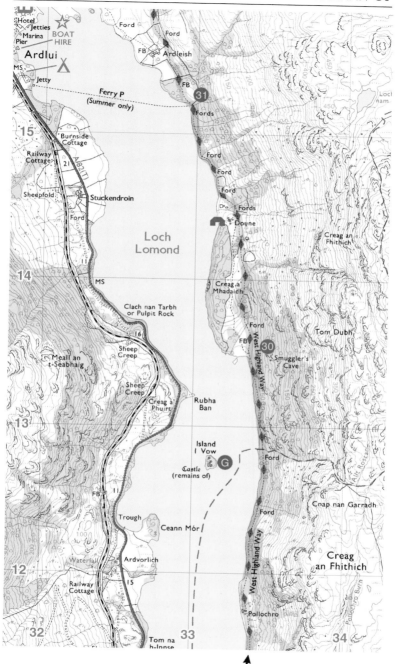

Gorse brightens the hillside in late Spring as the Way enters Glen Falloch near Inverarnan.

a row of peaks that stand above the head of the loch, Ben Lui, Ben Oss and Beinn Dubhchraig. There is now the immediate promise of good, open walking, up a little glen surrounded by rock-strewn hills, while a stream gurgles noisily but invisibly in a deep gully by the track.

At the top of the hill **32** turn right onto the wooden walkway and steps that cover an area of peaty, marshy land. Then at the top of a slight rise the whole view opens out over the splendours of Glen Falloch. The way begins to go downhill past the ruins of an old shieling and there is a view over the great S-bend of the River Falloch. At one time boats used to come up the Falloch to this point and then continue along a short artificial canal that delivered guests to the Inverarnon Hotel **H**. The path enters an area of storm-devastated woodland, and soon begins to go quite steeply down as a stony track through the trees. It eventually arrives at the flat floor of the glen in a marshy area spiked with reeds. This section ends at the footbridge over the Ben Glas Burn **33**. Many walkers, however, will want to visit Inverarnan. They should turn left to follow the path down to the river then right along the riverbank to the bridge, cross the bridge and turn left at the road. One attraction is the eighteenth-century Drovers Inn, a splendidly eccentric establishment where the visitor is greeted by a hall full of stuffed animals and birds, including a somewhat moth-eaten bear, and an old dummy dressed up as a red-coated soldier. Return by the same route to continue the walk.

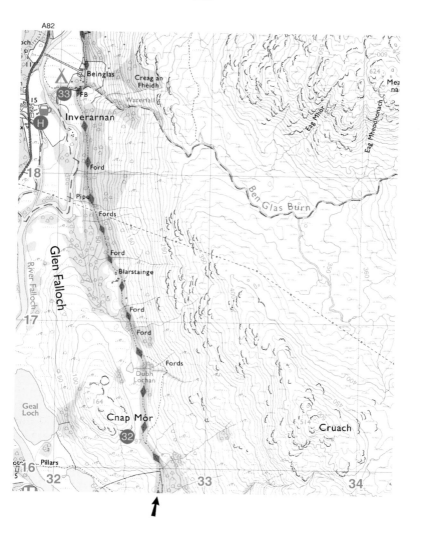

A succession of falls large and small mark the course of the River Falloch and add a special attraction to this section of the walk.

4 INVERARNAN TO TYNDRUM

via Glen Falloch and Crianlarich   *12 miles (19 km)*

This seems a comfortably easy section after the rigours of Loch Lomond, and although some of the route is shared with the road and rail traffic, they are seldom intrusive. Across the bridge **33** by the old Beinglas Farm is bunkhouse accommodation with some very strange new structures, whose name exactly conveys what they look like – wooden wigwams. Turn right over the bridge and follow the path round the bunkhouses to join a broader track. From here one gets an early glimpse of the railway crossing a gulley on the far side of the valley by a lattice girder bridge. After climbing a slight incline the track drops back down to the river with the main road beside it. This is a most attractive area with woodland still dominated by oak, through which run a number of streams crossed by bridges. The path narrows as it comes down to the river which roars down a rocky gorge in a series of waterfalls **A**. These are the start of the Falloch falls that make this riverside walk so exciting. Even moving away from the river into the birch woodland, the falls are not left behind, for a tributary stream plunges down beneath a wooden bridge. Then the path climbs again, providing a wider vista of the River Falloch, with Beinn Dubhchraig rearing up behind it. Dropping down, the wide view is lost but yet another set of falls appear as compensation. After that the river becomes strangely placid as it meanders through the fields.

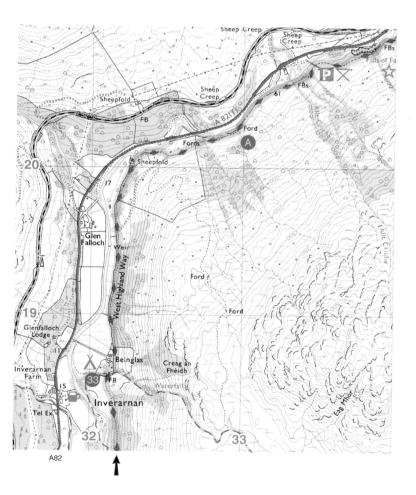

A82

The Way follows the line of the old military road as it begins the climb out of Glen Falloch.

The walking becomes pleasant and easy, if a little too close to the noise of the road traffic for comfort. The path narrows down to a few inches in width then crosses a stile **34** and continues on the soft turf of a field – a rare treat on this walk. The route continues by the river, then follows round the edge of the field to the footbridge **35**, after which it becomes a broad track that heads briefly uphill before descending again to the neat, single-storey, whitewashed farm of Derrydaroch **B** and the bridge over the river. This is a delightful spot where the tumbling river has carved deep hollows in the rocks filled with beautiful, clear water.

Cross over the bridge and immediately turn right onto the gravel path. Although the road is again near at hand, it is well shielded as the Way wanders through a patch of birch wood. There are still more falls to enjoy and the path climbs a little hill which provides a fine view back down the glen. The railway announces its presence with the appearance of a rusty broken-down waggon beside the walk. The path now turns to go through the railway embankment via a sheep creep **36** which may be comfortable for sheep, but is a good deal less so for human beings, forced to bend double with packs scraping the roof.

Once under the railway, ignore the steps and follow the track round to the right, cross the stream and continue on what was the main road before the new section was built. Go under the new road in the tunnel, and continue on the path that goes very steeply uphill. Where it joins the broad track turn right. The Way is now once again back with one of the old eighteenth-century military roads.

The path continues uphill, but now on an altogether gentler gradient, and as it climbs past the farm it becomes decidedly rougher, in places churned up by cattle. As the track levels out a large conifer plantation can be seen up ahead. This is entered via a kissing gate **37**. Three paths meet here. Those who wish to visit Crianlarich should take the path to the right, and can join the main route via a waymarked path from the village. The path straight ahead leads down to Bogle Glen, but the main West Highland Way route swings away to the left. A look at the map suggests that the next couple of miles are going to be spent in a dense plantation, but happily this is very far from being the case. The Way takes a rather tortuous route, turning this way and that, uphill and down again, ensuring a constantly changing scene.

The path climbs to a grassy summit and a magnificent viewpoint **C**. Straight ahead massive Ben More rises to a height of 3821 feet (1165 metres) while down below the River Fillan wends its way along the valley, crossed at Crianlarich by the Glenbruar Viaduct carrying the railway on towards Fort William. This is a pleasant spot to pause, admire the view and contemplate the fact that roughly half the Way has now been completed. The path disappears temporarily into the trees but these soon clear to a delightful heather-covered hillside and more views down Strath Fillan. It is worth looking up as well as down,

The view from the bridge across the River Fillan.

for this is a popular spot for gently gliding buzzards. The path now goes downhill quite steeply to a footbridge over a burn, which splashes down over a series of rock ledges. On the other side of the bridge, the trees begin to close in for the first time, cutting off the wider view. The path immediately climbs again to reach a track **38**. Turn right onto this broader path, which soon becomes a very stony way heading down towards the valley floor. Where the track turns sharply to the right **39** turn left onto the narrow path which follows the bank of a little burn down to the railway viaduct **D**. This is not a

This typical small hill farm stands close to the ruins of the medieval priory of St

The Priory of St Fillan may have long since become disused, but the graveyard remains and is still maintained.

girder viaduct like all the others seen so far along the Way, but a rather handsome stone structure. There is a simple explanation – it is not the same line. This is the old Caledonian Railway route to Oban. It runs to the south of the Fillan, while the West Highland runs to the north, the two bitter rivals glaring at each other across the water.

Go under the viaduct and turn left onto the old road, now running alongside the busy new carriageway. At the end of the tarmac section continue in the same direction through a copse of young birch trees. Where the path ends **40** cross straight over the road and follow the continuation of the path directly opposite. Turn right over the stile to cross the bridge over the river. There is now a break from the rough terrain and steep tracks of the hills, and an easy walk through rich riverside meadows. Turn left in front of the farmhouse **41** after which the path arrives at two small graveyards and the scant remains of St Fillan's Priory **E**. St Fillan was an Irish monk who preached Christianity to the scattered communities of the Highlands in the eighth century. Tradition has it that this was the site of Fillan's own simple chapel, which developed into a small monastery and was raised to the status of a priory by Robert the Bruce. Although the priory has gone, the site has retained its special significance for local Christians, which explains the two neat, well-maintained graveyards. Turn left by the priory and continue on the track at the foot of the hill. At Auchtertyre Farm **42**, glance up the side valley to see the West Highland railway crossing above the falls of the stream. There is also another set of wooden wig-wams, like those met at the beginning of this section. Cross over the river and follow the track round to the left heading back to the main road, for the end of this little diversion.

Go straight across the road, go over the stile and take the track beside the river. The rich pasture has now been left behind and rougher grazing has taken its place. The river is spanned by a fine old stone bridge, but the path remains on the same bank. Cross straight over the old road and continue along the riverside walk to a confused area of gravel and hummocks, representing the erosion of material carried down during the last glaciation. At the pebbly beach **43** turn right on to the narrow path that runs between the trees and the fence. The path swings away from the River Cononish, turning left then left again on to a broad track then left once more to cross the tributary stream. The water plunges down a rocky gully, just one more to add to the list of attractive falls that have been such a feature of this section of the walk.

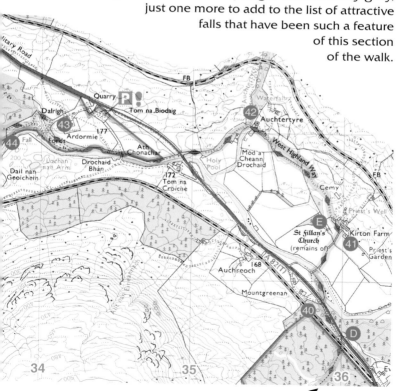

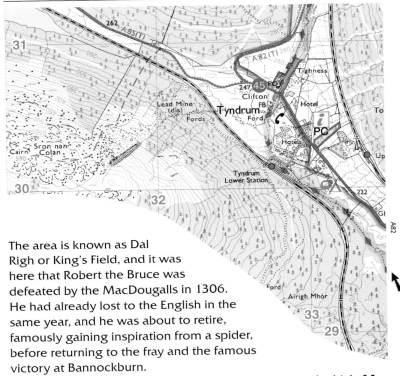

The area is known as Dal Righ or King's Field, and it was here that Robert the Bruce was defeated by the MacDougalls in 1306. He had already lost to the English in the same year, and he was about to retire, famously gaining inspiration from a spider, before returning to the fray and the famous victory at Bannockburn.

The track now continues past a lochan, just beyond which **44** a much narrower path turns off to the right. It wriggles away across an area of peaty moorland dotted with conifers while the burn follows an equally erratic course over to the right. Going through the gate, take the path to the left that wanders through the attractive pine forest. It approaches quite close to the railway – the Oban line again this time – then drops down to the bank of the burn. It passes a caravan park and the road that leads down to the rather grand Royal Hotel. The path, however, continues past Tyndrum lower station and on through a gate, to stay with the stream before turning on to the road running past the neat rows of cottages that make up Clifton village **45**. This village was created to house workers from the lead mines opened up along the upper reaches of the Cononish River in the mid-eighteenth century which were worked intermittently for the next hundred years. There was a smelting works near the village at the edge of the woodland. Follow the road down to the main road at the edge of Tyndrum: shops, a hotel and café can be found along this road to the right.

The falls with their surroundings of birch and heather are an attractive feature of the approach to Tyndrum.

5 TYNDRUM TO KINGSHOUSE

via Bridge of Orchy and Inveroran   *18½ miles (30 km)*

This is the longest section of the Way, but almost all of the walking is on good, sound tracks and comparatively easy. On the other hand, it has on offer some of the finest wild scenery of the entire route, which on a good day tempts the contemplative lingerer. In bad weather, however, the fine scenery may be a good deal less appreciated, for there is very little in the way of shelter anywhere along this part of the walk. Fortunately, it is possible to make a break at either Bridge of Orchy or Inveroran and indeed, many walkers prefer to break this section into two stages, spread out over a couple of days.

At the end of the road through Clifton village, cross straight over the A82 and continue on the track opposite. It is immediately obvious from the roughly cobbled surface that this is an old road, and it is in fact another section of the eighteenth-century military road, which will form the basis of the West Highland Way for many miles.

The track soon comes back to run alongside the main road, which is now also heading north. A group of startlingly blue tanks serve as reservoirs for the Tyndrum water supply. Here the valley has narrowed down so that all the transport routes – old military road, modern trunk road and railway are squeezed together in the gap. The Way crosses the burn on an attractive arched stone bridge and then goes over the railway on a more utilitarian, angular structure **46** before continuing on in the same direction. The shapely cone of Beinn Odhar dominates the view up ahead. Immediately beyond a metal gate **47**, turn off the military road on to a narrow path that climbs up the hillside for a little way and then levels out to follow the contours. The path then drops down again, goes under the railway **48** and then turns right back on to the original broad track. By now the main road has slid away to the west and is shielded by a patch of woodland. This section of the old road runs on an artificial terrace carved out of the hillside, with a steep rock-strewn slope to the right, and the river making its lazy way along the valley to the left. Up ahead the mountains of Glencoe are already coming into view.

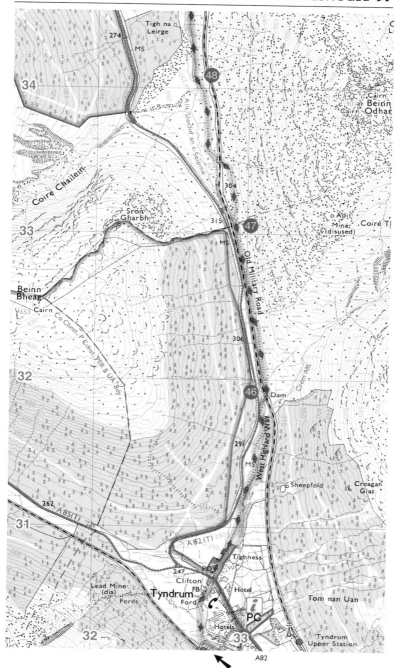

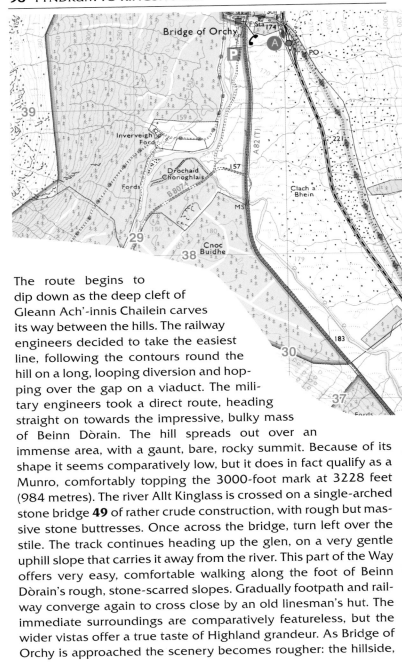

The route begins to dip down as the deep cleft of Gleann Ach'-innis Chailein carves its way between the hills. The railway engineers decided to take the easiest line, following the contours round the hill on a long, looping diversion and hopping over the gap on a viaduct. The military engineers took a direct route, heading straight on towards the impressive, bulky mass of Beinn Dòrain. The hill spreads out over an immense area, with a gaunt, bare, rocky summit. Because of its shape it seems comparatively low, but it does in fact qualify as a Munro, comfortably topping the 3000-foot mark at 3228 feet (984 metres). The river Allt Kinglass is crossed on a single-arched stone bridge **49** of rather crude construction, with rough but massive stone buttresses. Once across the bridge, turn left over the stile. The track continues heading up the glen, on a very gentle uphill slope that carries it away from the river. This part of the Way offers very easy, comfortable walking along the foot of Beinn Dòrain's rough, stone-scarred slopes. Gradually footpath and railway converge again to cross close by an old linesman's hut. The immediate surroundings are comparatively featureless, but the wider vistas offer a true taste of Highland grandeur. As Bridge of Orchy is approached the scenery becomes rougher: the hillside, faced with crags, dangles down long grey beards of scree. The path eventually turns back down to the railway at Bridge of Orchy station **A**. There are neat little buildings in a cosy, cottage style of the sort that used to feature on old-fashioned toy train sets. It is almost as if the architect had given up all attempts to match his buildings to the scenery and had settled for something that would have fitted equally well in Surbiton or Bagshot.

Immediately beyond the station, cross the line by the subway and follow the station approach road down to the A82, close by the popular Bridge of Orchy Hotel. Walkers not pausing for refreshment should cross straight over the main road on to the minor road that crosses the river on the Bridge of Orchy itself. This is the most elegant of the military bridges met along the Way, built around 1750 to the design of Major William Caulfield who took over the task of road construction in the Highlands from General Wade. Immediately beyond the bridge **50** turn left off the tarmac road on to the narrow path that climbs up through the trees. Rather surprisingly, perhaps, this is still on the line of the military road. Why the easy route used by the modern road was not followed instead is something of a mystery – and must have been even more bewildering to the redcoats toiling up the hill with full packs and guns. This is a good uphill slog through the pine forest, but one that

The Bridge of Orchy, built around 1750, is one of the most imposing features of the old military road.

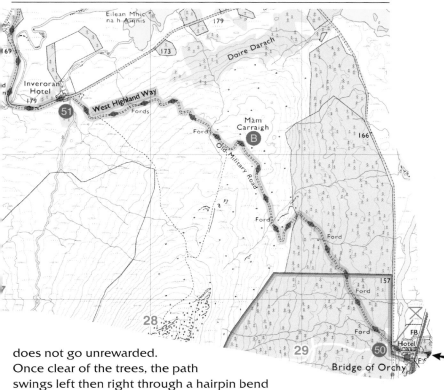

does not go unrewarded.
Once clear of the trees, the path
swings left then right through a hairpin bend
to reach the crest of the hill **B**. It is a modest summit
just topping the thousand-foot mark, but the view is as good as
any on the whole walk. The hill is surrounded on all sides by
mountain peaks, with Loch Tulla and the wilderness of Rannoch
Moor stretching out in front. Having reached the top, the Way
heads downhill in a series of extravagant zig-zags, while the cries
of curlews drift up from the moorland round the loch.

At the road **51** turn left past another popular stopping place,
the Inveroran Hotel. The remainder of this section lies across the
edge of Rannoch Moor. It is the wildest part of the whole Way and
needs to be treated with respect, for there is no shelter and no
escape from whatever the weather chooses to throw at the
walker. The author remembers, all too clearly, walking this way
some years earlier with a gale-force wind driving sleeting rain
straight into the face. It was not an enjoyable experience. Yet it is
precisely this wildness that also makes this one of the most
rewarding sections of the whole Way.

Sullen skies add sombre tones to the wilderness of Rannoch Moor near Ba Bridg

ckdrop of hills.

The beginning is unassuming, a stroll down the road past a clump of pines and a simple wooden bungalow. Then the essential character of the moor begins to assert itself, as the road swings round to enter an area of peaty bog, with clusters of tall pine trees. It passes above the rough marshy land at the head of Loch Tulla, to cross the river at Victoria Bridge. Immediately beyond that is Forest Lodge **52**, where the military road diverges from the Way, which carries straight on along an old drove road. This heads off through the pinewoods as a roughly cobbled track with drainage ditches and stone walls on either side. It emerges into the open to run alongside a conifer plantation, brightened at the edge by clumps of rhododendrons. On the right the entrance to the driveway leading down to Black Mount Lodge is marked by the ruins of an old gatehouse which must once have been a rather jolly piece of mock-baronial architecture.

For a time the Way climbs steadily with the plantation to one side, and grassy hummocks and heather to the other. It is only when the trees come to an end that one begins to get a notion of the awesome emptiness of Rannoch Moor. Surrounded by hills, it is a landscape of rough humps emerging from a wilderness of brown, peat-stained pools, rough grass and heather. It is obvious why some sort of surfaced track was needed, whether for drovers or soldiers, for to stray from the path by only a few paces in any direction is to find oneself in a squelchy quagmire. Where drainage channels have been cut it is possible to see just how the thin layer of vegetation rests on a great mass of black peat. Here and there the bleached stumps of old trees poke out as dead reminders of the ancient living forest.

The track eventually levels out and offers a view across the wide expanses of Loch Tulla. Rannoch Moor is often described as 'empty', but that might suggest that it lacks interest. Exactly the opposite is true: this is an area of constantly changing patterns, where the emphasis shifts all the time between the immediate surroundings and the wider vistas. At first the horizon is dominated by the two shapely hills that make up Black Mount, but equally appealing is the little stream that dances down from the heights of Beinn Toaig to pass under the low stone bridge **C** close by the next conifer plantation. A second plantation is passed on the right and the view changes again, and now one is faced with the moor at its wildest. A reedy lochan is surrounded by a landscape of pools and humps, where white spears of grass thrust out among patches of heather. It is here that one really appreciates

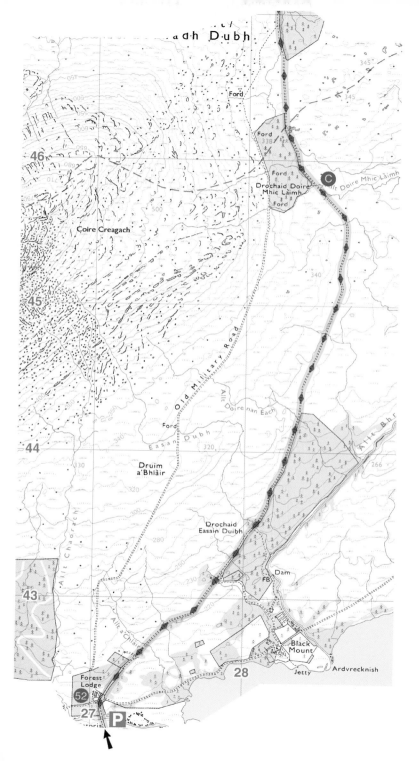

that this is the edge of the moor as the hills of Coire Bà form a margin to the west, while the wild country stretches to far horizons to the east. If there is any one place that tempts the walker to pause on a good day it is Bà Bridge **D**. Here the River Bà gallops down from the hills in a tumble of water and rocks. Upstream is the vast amphitheatre of the Coire with its semi-circle of rocky peaks; downstream is the peat moor, a confusion of streams and lochans. The only false note is struck by the small plantation, surely one of the most insensitive pieces of planting ever imposed on a wilderness area. It is easy to linger, and it is not difficult to see why many walkers allow a whole day to take in this section from Bridge of Orchy or Inveroran. There are a number of little bridges over burns where anyone could happily sit and contemplate the scene, look out for birds or perhaps a herd of deer on the hills – or simply do nothing at all except enjoy the peace and solitude and the constant change of pattern and colour as sunlight alternates with cloud shadows.

Leaving the bridge, the track passes the ruins of lonely Bà Cottage and begins to climb to a new summit, marked by a cairn on a hillock to the left **E**. The track now swings round the shoulder

Loch Tulla near Victoria Bridge, marking the start of the walk across the open spaces of Rannoch Moor.

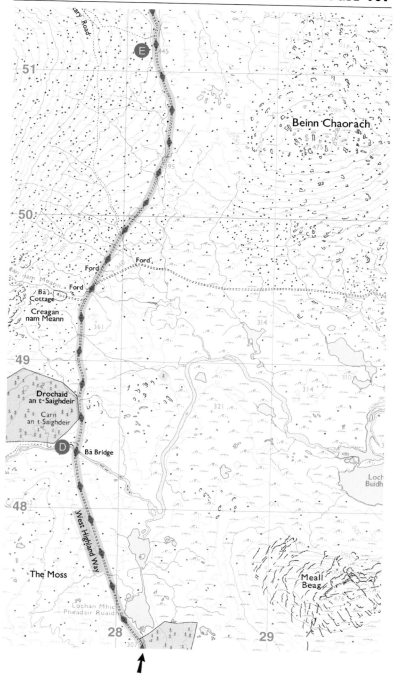

Beinn Chaorach

Ford
Ford
Ford
Bà
Cottage
Creagan
nam Meann

Drochaid
an t-Saighdeir
Carn
an t-Saighdeir

Bà Bridge

West Highland Way

The Moss

Meall
Beag

Loch
Buidh

Lochan Mhic
Pheadair Ruaidh

The old Blackrock Cottage, now a mountain hut, and behind it Buachaille Etive

...ding guardian over the Pass of Glencoe.

Looking across Loch Tulla to Black Mount, and the West Highland Way that runs just beyond the trees.

of the hill and as it does so a whole immense new panorama opens out, encompassing the moor, the distant Grampian Mountains beyond it and the hills of Glencoe, dominated by one of Britain's most beautiful and shapely mountains, Buachaille Etive Mór. The track now goes downhill to join the roadway to the White Corries Ski Lift **53**. At the Ski Centre to the left there is a museum devoted to the history of mountaineering and ski-ing in the region, but the Way turns right towards the main road. It passes the attractive, whitewashed Blackrock Cottage, run as a mountain hut by the Ladies' Scottish Climbing Club. Close by the track is a peaty bog with a mass of tree stumps.

Cross over the road **54** and continue straight on along the minor road. From here Buachaille Etive Mór can be seen as an almost perfectly shaped cone presenting an imposing face of sheer rock. It stands at a junction of two glens – Glen Etive runs away enticingly below the southern flank of the mountain, while Glencoe leads away to the west. It is not just the memories of the massacre that give Glencoe its sombre air. It is tightly shut in between tall hills, and clouds often form a roof between them so that the road seems to be vanishing into a dark tunnel. It also, however, offers some of the most exhilarating mountain scenery in Britain, and walkers with time to spare will find an expedition up the glen very rewarding. This section ends at the Kingshouse Hotel **55**, sitting snugly behind its shield of conifers. The hotel has been here for at least two centuries, at first serving the varied needs of honest drovers and less honest smugglers. Those who stop here and linger on in the morning will find deer wandering down off the hills to breakfast on the hotel's left-overs.

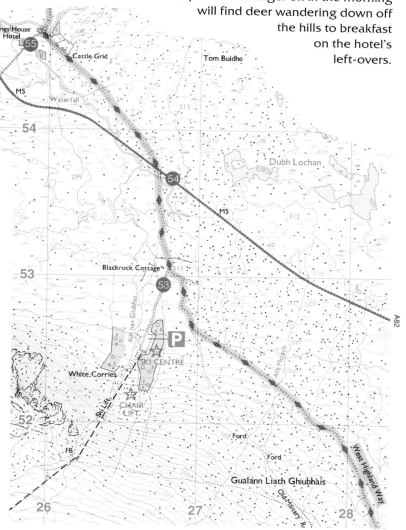

The shapely cone of Buachaille Etive Mór as seen from the Way near the Kings

6 KINGSHOUSE TO KINLOCHLEVEN

via the Devil's Staircase

9 miles (14.5 km)

Walkers who carry tents and food can enjoy a flexibility denied to others on the Way, for whom there is now just one place offering food and accommodation between here and the end of the walk at Fort William. Those who opt to do it all in a day need to be very fit, for it is not just a comparatively long walk, but one which includes the two most taxing climbs to the highest points on the whole journey. This account assumes that most walkers would prefer to break the walk at Kinlochleven, which still leaves a good day's hike for the finale.

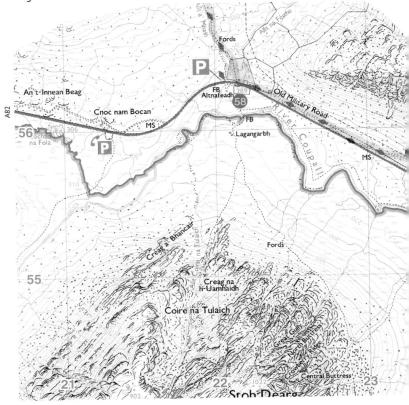

Cross over the bridge at Kingshouse **55** where a glance down into the water will reveal a large trout population. Like the local deer, the trout benefit from kitchen scraps, but fortunately for them, they are generally too small for the kitchen frying pan. Continue on the minor road, turning left at the fence **56**: this is in fact the original main road down Glencoe which also follows the track of the older military road. There is now a view straight down Glen Etive which pierces to the heart of a wild, mountainous region. The road begins to converge with the modern trunk road, but just before they meet, turn right over a stile **57** beside a metal gate and take the path up the hill. Having climbed up to a point satisfactorily distanced from the noise and fumes of traffic, the path at once begins to go down again, back to the A82. After negotiating the stony path over trickly hill streams, there is a short and unappealing walk right on the verge of the road. It comes as some relief to cross a stile and take a path that is at least separated a little from the traffic. The path arrives at a group of sheepfolds and there is a view down to the glen at the far side of Buachaille Etive Mór, with farmhouses dotted down under the shadows of the mountains. The path runs between the folds and the road, and briefly rejoins the road itself in front of the white house surrounded by pines. Immediately beyond the house **58** turn right on to the path, cross the footbridge over the stream and begin the climb out of Glencoe.

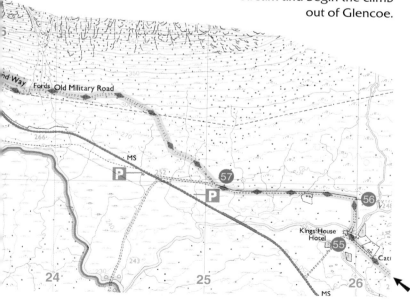

The view from the top of the Devil's Staircase, looking north with Ben Nevis in the distance.

This part of the route is known as the Devil's Staircase, but is not as fierce as its name suggests. The total climb is 849 feet (259 metres) but the gradient is never really severe. At first the path goes comparatively straight, running by a small, clear burn. Then as the hillside steepens, the track goes into a series of ever more extravagant zig-zags until a cairn announces that the summit has been reached. This is a moment to pause for a look back over the mountains of Glencoe, before walking on over the saddle between the two peaks **A** for a new vista of the mountains to the north. One peak, at least, is unmistakable, the vast, hunched-up shoulder of Ben Nevis.

After pausing to enjoy what is, on a clear day, one of the great views of the West Highland Way, continue on the same path that now begins the long, slow descent to Kinlochleven. Rounding the shoulder of the hill **B** there is a view eastward to Blackwater Reservoir. It was built between 1905 and 1909, one of the last great engineering works in Britain to rely mainly on the muscle power of thousands of navvies. It was constructed to supply water to what was at the time the biggest hydro-electric power scheme in the country. More details of the system emerge during the rest of this section of the walk, for soon the pipes can be seen that carry the water from the dam to Kinlochleven. Thoughts of industrial processes are soon driven away, however, by the delights of the hill scenery.

The path runs along a rock ledge on the side of the hill, from which one can look down and catch a first glimpse of houses far below. Then the path begins to twist down the hill with a view of the back of the hills that border Glencoe, and what looks a most enticing walk along the ridge. The path eventually comes down to a footbridge over a burn **59** before continuing to follow the contours round the next hillside. There is now an impressive view of

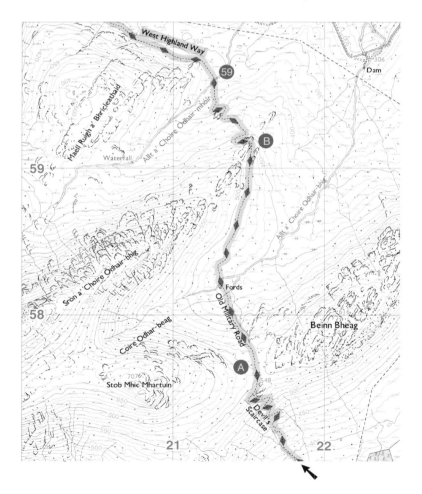

the pipes from the Blackwater Reservoir snaking across the land-scape. Other views have, however, been totally lost as Ben Nevis and the high mountains to the north disappear behind the hills that border Loch Leven. The path winds down towards woodland, beginning with a thin scattering of delicate silver birch. A pen-stock **C** appears which controls the flow of water along the final plunge to Kinlochleven: here excess water can be allowed to flow off, down to the River Leven. From this point, the Way follows the access road used by vehicles to reach the penstock.

The track heads down towards the loch, but where the pipeline makes the journey in about a mile (1.5 km) the track takes twice as long to reach the same point. It descends through the increasingly dense birch wood in a series of hairpin bends passing a small reser-voir. It is all a great contrast to the open hills and moor, as birdsong echoes among the trees. The Way crosses a stone bridge over a rocky gorge and a series of cascades, with the high wall of the dam visible a little way upstream **60**. The track now heads more gently, but more directly, downhill on the opposite side of the little valley. Here there is an excellent close-up of the six massive pipes that swoop down the hill like an immense fairground slide.

The path eventually emerges by a large industrial complex, the Kinlochleven aluminium smelter **D**. It was to power this complex

A small bridge crosses a stream on the way down to Kinlochleven.

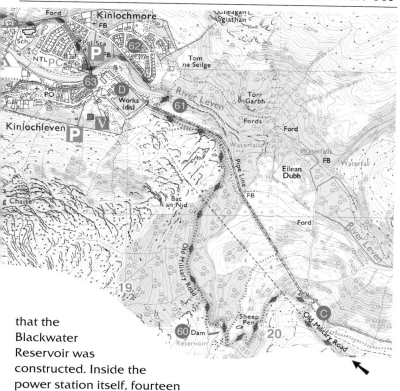

that the
Blackwater
Reservoir was
constructed. Inside the
power station itself, fourteen
turbines were installed, producing electricity for the works and
the surrounding area. Although smelting has ending, the power
station will continue in operation, sending electricity to the grid.
Kinlochleven itself was originally built as a 'model village' to house
the workforce brought to what was then a quiet spot at the head of
the sea loch. The path crosses the pipeline to run behind the smelter.
Where the path divides, carry straight on downhill to the bridge **61**
over the River Leven which runs through a medley of white and
salmon-pink rocks. The path swings round to the left to a little wood
then rejoins the road past quite surprisingly suburban houses.
Halfway down the road **62** turn left to join the riverside path. Here
the water that started its journey up at the dam gushes out into the
river with the immense force accumulated in the drop of around a
thousand feet. Immediately beyond the outflow, turn right to
rejoin the road **63**. Those stopping in Kinlochleven should turn left
for shops, café and pub and a museum and visitor centre, The
Aluminium Story. Those continuing on along the Way, turn right.

The view from the head of Loch Leven.

7 KINLOCHLEVEN TO FORT WILLIAM

via Glen Nevis

It is worth repeating that this is quite a long leg – and you can add another mile if you are continuing on from the official end of the walk to the centre of Fort William – and there are no facilities of any sort along the way. So it is essential that any supplies you need are with you before you set out.

The first section follows the road as it turns the head of the loch and follows the north shore. This was once busy with traffic, but since the ferry across the mouth of Loch Leven at North Ballachulish was replaced by a bridge it has become quite peaceful. At the school **64** turn right on to the track through the wood. This is still following the military road, though evidence of its nature is not always immediately obvious: one clue to look out for is the way in which stones have been set on stream beds to create smooth fords. This is an attractive route through woodland again dominated by birch. Just before reaching a small hill stream, the track divides **65**. Turn left to cross the stream. Just beyond a second stream, the path goes up quite steeply via a flight of rough stone steps. This is a hint of what is to come, for by the time the first summit is reached it will have climbed almost exactly the same height as the path up the Devil's Staircase from Glencoe – and this route is, if anything, rather harder going. The path now crosses over a roadway and continues on up the hill, soon beginning to zig-zag to ease the gradient. It then dips down slightly to a stream where there is a clearing in the birchwood, and a view down to the narrow, steep-sided inlet of Loch Leven. Another track now joins in from the left **66**, but the Way continues straight on. Beyond that there is another clearing, and at each gap the view goes on getting better and better. A section of recognisably made-up road swings round in a hairpin bend to emerge from the trees and now the whole view is clear. The most prominent features are the mountains to the south, marked at their westerly end by the shapely Pap of Glencoe. It is a view to rival that from the Devil's Staircase, and just as well-earned. At the summit knoll **A** a broad track appears from Mamore Lodge to the east and the way ahead takes on a very different aspect.

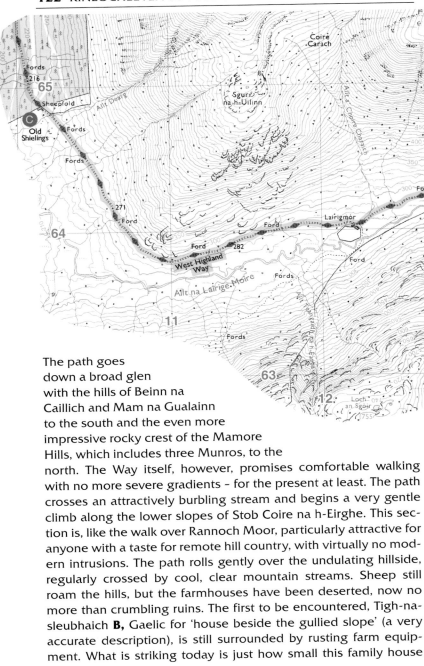

The path goes
down a broad glen
with the hills of Beinn na
Caillich and Mam na Gualainn
to the south and the even more
impressive rocky crest of the Mamore
Hills, which includes three Munros, to the
north. The Way itself, however, promises comfortable walking
with no more severe gradients – for the present at least. The path
crosses an attractively burbling stream and begins a very gentle
climb along the lower slopes of Stob Coire na h-Eirghe. This section is, like the walk over Rannoch Moor, particularly attractive for
anyone with a taste for remote hill country, with virtually no modern intrusions. The path rolls gently over the undulating hillside,
regularly crossed by cool, clear mountain streams. Sheep still
roam the hills, but the farmhouses have been deserted, now no
more than crumbling ruins. The first to be encountered, Tigh-na-
sleubhaich **B,** Gaelic for 'house beside the gullied slope' (a very
accurate description), is still surrounded by rusting farm equipment. What is striking today is just how small this family house

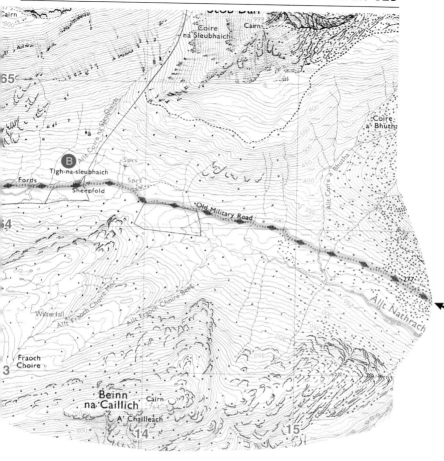

was, a testament to the hard work and poor returns of the hill farmers. The second, a little further along the way, is similar, built of sturdy stone to withstand harsh winters but with no hint of luxury.

The glen appears at first to be closed in by low hills to the west, but as the walker gets nearer it becomes clear that the whole valley is swinging round to the north. As the glen turns so the path begins a gentle climb up the shoulder of the hill. Then, as the corner is turned, woodland can be seen up ahead, and woodland is to provide the dominant theme for the rest of the way. The path passes old shielings **C** which provided temporary homes for the clansfolk during the summer grazing period in the hills. It continues through a complex of sheepfolds and enters the wood. The

The Way following the track of the old military road from Glencoe to Kinlochle...

Old farm machinery scattered over the valley floor near the abandoned farm of Tigh-na-sleubhaich.

path becomes a broad forest track, with the trees well set back so that it does not seem too claustrophobic, and firebreaks provide brief opportunities to enjoy the wider view. At the edge of the wood **67** turn off the forest track onto the narrower path to the right. Here a seat has been provided for those who would like to pause and enjoy the scenery. The end of Lochan Lùnn Dà-Bhrà can be seen, and for the first time since leaving Kinlochleven, a road. This is, in fact, following the line of the military road and provides an easy shorter walk into Fort William for anyone who needs it. The Way, however, now turns away from the old route for the very last time, and briefly plunges back into the woods.

Leave the woods by a very high stile **68** and climb straight up the small hill. This offers an even better view down over the whole of the lochan, in its setting of wild moorland and distant hills. The path now runs as a small terrace on the hillside with yet more dark woodland up ahead. But before the woods are reached the view opens out quite dramatically as Ben Nevis looms over the trees. The path now wriggles its way into the conifers, entering the woods via a wooden stile **69**. It crosses a mountain stream on a wooden bridge, and then heads straight on towards the mountain as if it were determined to keep going all the way to the summit. Another stile **70** is crossed to a patch of open ground, followed immediately by a return to the woods and what will turn out to be a very rugged section of walking. At first the going is easy, and the walker can enjoy birdsong and the company of remarkably tame chaffinches and thrushes. There is a pleasant, open feel to the walk and constant views of hills and mountains. Then the trees

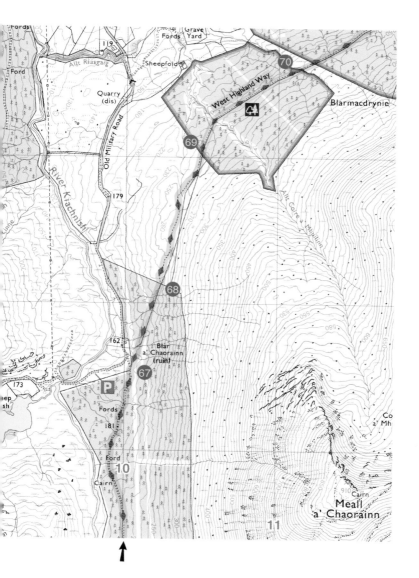

close in and the path plunges downhill with wooden stairs to help on the steepest section at the bottom. It ends with a bridge over a rocky gorge, where a stream, its banks dotted with silver birch, spalshes delicate green and white against the darker conifers. Now, inevitably, there is a climb up the other side, though the effort is eased by the enticing glimpses of mountain scenery through the trees. The gradient eases and the walk becomes a long, steady ascent, past a craggy ridge which pushes up above the trees that clamber up the slopes but stop just short of the summit. Throughout this section the path dips, rises and turns so that there is never any lack of interest along the way.

The forest track opens out to provide one of the more dramatic views of Ben Nevis.

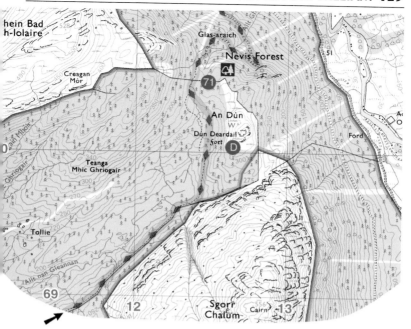

The Way reaches a fence **71** where a new path has been created to allow walkers to visit the Iron Age hill-fort of Dùn Deardail **D**. It is only a short detour and does provide an opportunity to see an archaeological curiosity. Hill-forts were common in Britain during the period which lasted from roughly 500 BC to the first century AD. Some were large enough to contain regular settlements, others simply places where people could retreat if attacked. Dùn Deardail is what is known as a vitrified fort, one in which the stone defences have been subjected to such intense heat that silicate materials in the rock, such as quartz, have melted to form a glassy mass. There are numerous theories as to how this happened, but the likeliest explanation is that the drystone walls that surrounded the summit were braced with timber cross-pieces. If these caught fire, intense heat would have been generated, causing vitrification. No one can now discover whether such fires were caused by accident or as part of an attack on the fort. From here there is a splendid view of Ben Nevis while down in the glen there is a glimpse of the houses on the outskirts of Fort William, indicating the end of the Way.

The nature of the walk now changes again, as it follows a broad track through the Nevis Forest. Much of the woodland has been felled, leaving scarred hillsides. Now the long descent to the bottom of Glen Nevis begins with great sweeping bends. The hillside above the walk is laced by streams, while down below a narrow strip of green fields separates the woodland from the lower slopes of Ben Nevis. Where the track reaches a gentler slope **72** a second track appears on the right, doubling back to the Youth Hostel and the road up Glen Nevis. The main route continues straight ahead to a point where a narrow path crosses the track **73**. Turn right to go steeply downhill; and where the path immediately divides, take the fork to the left. The conifers are now left behind for an area of deciduous woodland bordering a stream, which makes a pleasant change. It zig-zags down past a small cemetery. Go through the wooden gate at the edge of the wood and carry straight on down the track to the road **74**. Turn left and stay on the road to the end of the walk. It is a somewhat disappointing finale to an invigorating trek through wild country to end on a pavement beside a road, but there are things of interest along the way. A vast roadside boulder is described as a Counsel or Wishing Stone. There are various legends attached to the stone, including one that claims that at certain times the whole rock magically rotates and settles down again. It will, of course, only perform when no one is there to see it. Falls on the river form an attractive feature, but the outskirts of Fort William, when they appear, are not very prepossessing. On arriving at a roundabout **75**, proceed to Nevis Bridge, which crosses the river and marks the official end of the West Highland Way. The centre of Fort William is reached by carrying straight on down the road.

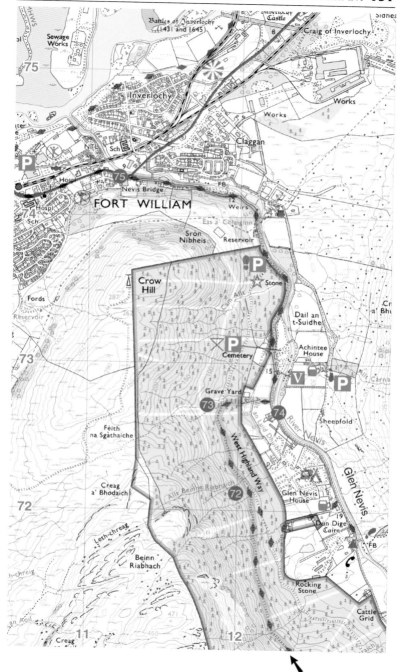

THE ASCENT OF BEN NEVIS

12½ miles (18km) return trip   *(see map on pages 134-5*

There are some who feel that though the West Highland Way is a magnificent walk, the end comes as an anti-climax. This need not be so, for anyone with a day to spare can, in the right conditions, add their own climax, with an ascent of Britain's highest mountain, Ben Nevis. But this is one of those climbs that needs to be taken seriously. In good weather, all that is needed is the stamina for the long haul to the summit. In winter – and winter on Ben Nevis can begin in October and last right through to May – only properly equipped and experienced mountaineers should attempt it. Even in high summer there are potential dangers. Weather changes very rapidly in this part of the world, and a walk that begins in sunshine can end with cloud covering the mountain and driving rain. The ascent up the obvious track may be simple enough, but once the top has been reached it is essential to locate the same route down again. It is easy in bad weather to roam the summit plateau and lose all sense of direction, and there are crags and steep falls for the unwary. Map and compass are, as always, the essential tools of the hill walker; and provided one knows how to use them and is suitably equipped for the walk, there should be few problems. The first essential is to check local weather forecasts and then prepare accordingly.

There are two starting places for walkers on the West Highland Way. The most popular route takes the bridge that crosses the river near the Visitor Centre, and takes the linking path to Achintee Farm, which offers bunkhouse accommodation. From here there is a clear track all the way to the summit. This bridleway was first constructed in 1883 to provide access to a weather observatory, so it takes the easiest line, offering a steady but never excessively steep climb. It passes beneath the face of Meall an t-Suidhe, then swings left to climb up Red Burn Gully, near the top of which it again swings round to the left to provide a more comfortable ascent. It emerges by a lochan, sitting in a hollow halfway up the mountain.

The path now crosses the Red Burn and then proceeds to zigzag its way to the summit plateau. It does not feel like a summit, more a bewildering, rocky wilderness, marked by the ruins of the observatory, abandoned in 1904, and the Peace Cairn, built to commemorate those who died in the Second World War. Again it is important to stress that there are dangers here, sharp drops and snow cornices that can last well into late spring, but common sense is the main defence against accidents. Do not stray too close to the edges, especially in bad weather, and be very sure that a patch of snow covers solid rock and not empty air. The descent follows exactly the same route back down again.

The alternative starting point is the Glen Nevis Youth Hostel. Cross the footbridge over the river opposite the hostel and follow the very obvious path that zig-zags up the steep hillside. It joins the bridleway on the rocky slope of Meall an t-Suidhe and then follows the route already described.

Is this a more appropriate end to the West Highland Way than a suburban traffic island? That is up to the individual to decide. Some will say that the ascent of Ben Nevis is little more than a hard, unremitting slog with little in the way of scenic delights when the top is finally reached; others would argue that to climb Britain's highest mountain is its own reward. But whichever ending is selected, busy Fort William or wild Ben Nevis, nothing can take away from the satisfaction and delights of one of Britain's greatest long-distance walks.

The West Highland Way stays on the valley floor, but Ben Nevis offers a more challenging grand finale to the walk.

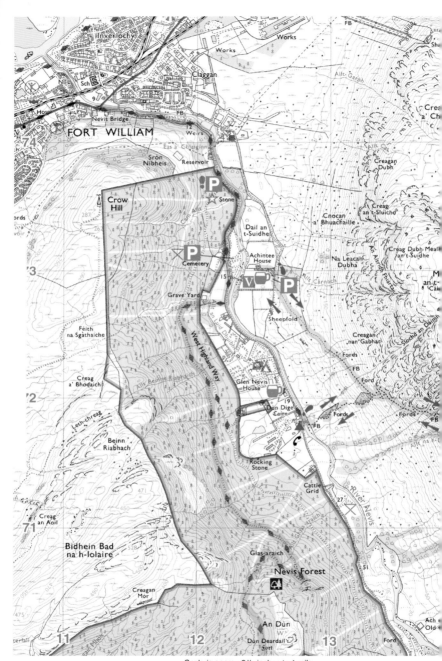

Scale is approx 2¼ inches to 1 mile

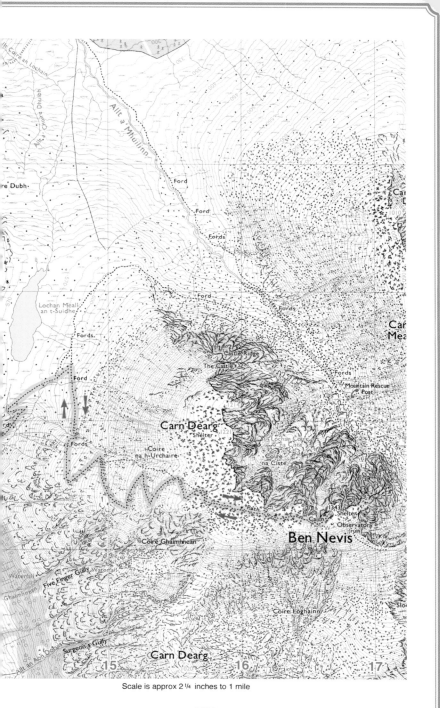

Scale is approx 2 ¼ inches to 1 mile

135

USEFUL
INFORMATION

TRANSPORT

Information on transport can be obtained from Tourist Information Centres in Scotland. There are also rail and coach centres which will be able to give specific information on timetables.

Rail Enquiries
National Rail Travel Passenger Enquiries (tel. 08457 484950, www.nationalrail.co.uk)

Coach Enquiries
National Express (tel. 08705 808080, www.gobycoach.com)

Getting to the start of the West Highland Way at Milngavie
If you are walking from the south to the north you will have a choice of transport to Milngavie. A regular rail service operates from the main line termini at Glasgow Queen Street Station or Central Station. Journey time is approximately 20 minutes. There is a frequent bus service from Buchanan Street Bus Station in Glasgow.

Returning to the start from Fort William after your walk
It is possible to return to Glasgow by rail or by coach from Fort William.

Passenger Ferry Services on Loch Lomond
There are a number of ferry services operating between Tarbet, Rowardennan, Inverbeg, Inversnaid and Inveruglas. Please contact Cruise Loch Lomond (tel. 01301 702356) or Rowardennan Hotel (tel. 01360 870273)
Inversnaid to Inveruglas
Daily sailings March to December, 8.30am and 5pm. Contact Inversnaid Hotel (tel. 01877 386223)

Ardleish to Ardlui
April to October, summon from shore by raising ball up the signal mast between the hours of operation: April, September and October, 9.30am to 7pm; May to August, 9.30am to 8pm.
Out of season by arrangement, contact Ardlui Hotel (tel. 01301 704243).

Boat Trips
Balmaha Boatyard, McFarlane & Son (tel. 01360 870214): sailings to Inchcailloch Nature Reserve Island and daily cruises

ACCOMMODATION

There is a good deal of information on the website www.west-highland-way.co.uk. West Highland Wayfarer is a holiday freesheet produced by Famedram Publishers Ltd. Send s.a.e. to PO Box 3, Ellon AB41 9EA .
It is also available on line at www.westhighlandwayfarer.co.uk

Youth Hostels
Rowardennan, by Drymen, Glasgow G63 0AR, tel. 01360 870259, GR 359992
Crianlarich, Station Road, FK20 8QN, tel. 01838 300260, GR 386250
Glen Nevis, Fort William PH33 6SY, tel. 01397 702336, GR 127716

Further information can be obtained from Scottish Youth Hostels Association at 7 Glebe Crescent, Stirling FK8 2JA (tel. 0845 2937373, www.syha.org.uk)

There are **bothies** at:
Rowchoish GR 336044
Doune GR 333145

TOURIST INFORMATION CENTRES

Visit Scotland, Old Town Jail, St John
Street, Stirling FK8 1EA,
tel. 01786 445222

Fort William Tourist Board, Cameron
Centre, Cameron Square
PH33 6AJ, tel. 01397 703781

Glasgow Tourist Board, 11 George
Square, G2 1DY, tel. 0141 204440

Summer only

Balloch, Balloch Road, G83 8LQ,
tel. 08707 200607

Drymen, The Library, The Square,
G63 0BD, tel. 08707 200611

Tarbet, Main Street, G83 7DE,
tel. 08707 200623

Tyndrum, Main Street, FK20 8RY

USEFUL ADDRESSES

British Trust for Ornithology, The
Nunnery, Thetford, Norfolk
IP24 2PU, tel. 01842 750050,
www.bto.org

Forestry Commission, Silvan House,
231 Corstorphine Road, Edinburgh
EH12 7AT, tel. 0845 3673787,
www.forestry.gov.uk

Historic Scotland, Longmore House,
Salisbury Place, Edinburgh
EH9 1SH, tel. 0131 6688600,
www.historic-scotland.gov.uk

National Trust for Scotland, Weymss
House, 28 Charlotte Square,
Edinburgh EH1 4ET, tel. 0844
4932100, www.nts.org.uk

Ordnance Survey, Romsey Road,
Maybush, Southampton
SO16 4GU, tel. 08456 050505,
www.ordnancesurvey.co.uk

The Ramblers Association Scotland,
Kingfisher House, Auld Mart
Business Park, Milnathort, Kinross
KY13 9DA, tel. 01577 861222,
www.ramblers.org.uk/scotland

**Royal Society for the Protection of
Birds**, www.rspb.org.uk

Scottish Natural Heritage, Great Glen
House, Leachkin Road, Inverness
IV3 8NW, tel. 01463 725000,
www.snh.org.uk

Scottish Wildlife Trust, Cramond
House, 3 Kirk Cramond, Cramond
Grebe Road, Edinburgh EH4 6HZ,
tel 0131 3127765, www.swt.org.uk

Weathercall (Meteorological Office)
Highlands and Islands,
tel. 09068 500425
Central Scotland and Strathclyde,
tel. 09068 500421

WEST HIGHLAND WAY COUNTRYSIDE RANGER SERVICE

Countryside Rangers and
Wardens operate along the
way. They will provide advice
and information to walkers
who are planning to walk the
route and also to those
actually using the Way. They
can be contacted at:

West Highland Way Ranger, Loch Lomond &
The Trossachs National Park, Carrochan
Road, Balloch G83 8EG, tel. 01389
722600, www.west-highland-way.co.uk.

Countryside Ranger Service, Highland
Council, Ionad Nibheis, Glen Nevis, Fort
William PH33 6PF, tel. 01397 705922,
e-mail westhighlandway@highland.gov.uk

ORDNANCE SURVEY MAPS COVERING THE WEST HIGHLAND WAY

Landranger Maps (scale 1:50000) 41, 50, 56, 57, 64

Explorer Maps (scale 1:25000) 342, 347, 348, 364, 377, 384, 385, 392

Bibliography

Buchan, John *The Massacre of Glencoe*, 1933, Buchan & Enwright 1985

Gillen, Con *Geology and Landscape of Scotland*, Terra, 2003

Haldane, A.R.B. *The Drove Roads of Scotland*, 1973, Birlinn 1998

Holden, Peter & Housden, Stuart *RSPB Handbook of Scottish Birds*, Christopher Helm, 2009

McCall, Colin *Routes, Roads, Regiments and Rebellions, a brief history of the life and work of General George Wade* 2003, Solcol

Thomas, John & Paterson, Alan *The West Highland Railway* House of Lochnar, 1998

Places to Visit on or near the West Highland Way

Glasgow
Art Gallery and Museum
Botanic Gardens
Burrell Collection
Clydebuilt at Braehead
Gallery of Modern Art
Glasgow Cathedral and Necropolis
Glasgow Science Centre
Hunterian Art Gallery
Hunterian Museum
Museum of Transport
Peoples' Palace
Pollok House (NTS)
The Riverside Museum and Tall Ship
The Tenement House (NTS)

Lillie Art Gallery, Milngavie
Mugdock Country Park
Glengoyne distillery
Loch Lomond National Park Centre, Balmaha
Queen Elizabeth Forest Park
Inversnaid RSPB Nature Reserve

Glencoe
Visitor Centre (NTS)*
Ski Centre*
Glencoe and North Lorn Folk Museum*

Aluminium Story Visitor Centre and Library, Kinlochleven
Glen Nevis Visitor Centre

Fort William
Jacobite Steam Train
West Highland Museum

Corpach
Caledonian Canal*
Treasures of the Earth*

Ben Nevis Distillery, Lochy Bridge*
Inverlochy Castle*

NTS is National Trust for Scotland

* Off route

ORDNANCE SURVEY MAPS COVERING THE WEST HIGHLAND WAY

Landranger Maps

(scale 1:50 000)
41, 50, 56, 57, 64

Explorer Maps

(scale 1:25 000)
342, 347, 348, 364, 377, 384, 385, 392

BIBLIOGRAPHY

Buchan, John, *The Massacre of Glencoe*, 1933, Buchan & Enwright, 1985

Haldane, A.R.B., *The Drove Roads of Scotland*, David & Charles, 1973

Linklater, Magnus, *Massacre, The Story of Glencoe*, Collins, 1982

Millman, R.N., *The Making of the Scottish Landscape*, Batsford, 1975

Murray, W.H., *Rob Roy MacGregor: His Life and Times*, Drew, 1982

Taylor, William, *The Military Roads of Scotland*, David & Charles, 1976

Thomas, John, *The West Highland Railway*, David & Charles, 1984

Thom, Valerie, *Birds in Scotland*, Poyser, 1986

Weir, Tom, *The Scottish Lochs*, Constable, 1980

Whittow, John, *Geology and Scenery in Scotland*, Chapman & Hall, 1992

The Official Guides to all of

Cotswold Way
Anthony Burton

100 miles of quintessentially
English landscape

ISBN 978 1 84513 519 5

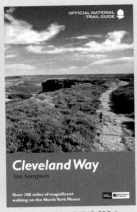

Cleveland Way
Ian Sampson

Over 100 miles of magnificent
walking on the North York Moors

ISBN 978 1 84513 520 1

Hadrian's Wall Path
Anthony Burton

Follow the Roman Wall
from coast to coast

ISBN 978 1 84513 567 6

Peddars Way and Norfolk Coast Path
Bruce Robinson

90 miles from Breckland to
salt marsh and sea cliffs

ISBN 978 1 84513 570 6

North Downs Way
Neil Curtis and Jim Walker

Follow the chalk ridge across South-East
England all the way to the sea

ISBN 978 1 84513 602 4

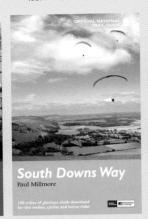

South Downs Way
Paul Millmore

100 miles of glorious chalk downland
for the walker, cyclist and horse rider

ISBN 978 1 84513 565 2

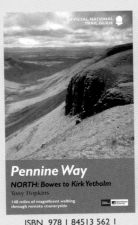

Pennine Way
NORTH: Bowes to Kirk Yetholm
Tony Hopkins

140 miles of magnificent walking
through remote countryside

ISBN 978 1 84513 562 1

Offa's Dyke Path
SOUTH: Chepstow to Knighton
Ernie and Kathy Kay and Mark Richards

Follow the ancient earthwork up the Wye
Valley and alongside the Black Mountains

ISBN 978 1 84513 561 4

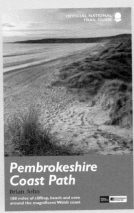

Pembrokeshire Coast Path
Brian John

180 miles of clifftop, beach and cove
around the magnificent Welsh coast

ISBN 978 1 84513 563 8

Britain's National Trails

South West Coast Path
Falmouth to Exmouth
Brian Le Messurier

172 miles of dramatic coves, cliffs and
beaches from Cornwall to Devon

ISBN 978 1 84513 564 5

Thames Path
David Sharp

Follow England's river all the way from its
peaceful source into the heart of the capital

ISBN 978 1 84513 566 9

The Ridgeway
Anthony Burton

87 miles of walking along the
crest of the downs

- ## Ordnance Survey mapping throughout
- ## Regularly and comprehensively revised
- ## Lavishly illustrated in full colour

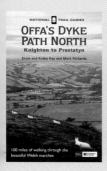

OFFA'S DYKE PATH NORTH
Knighton to Prestatyn
Ernie and Kathy Kay and Mark Richards

100 miles of walking through the
beautiful Welsh marches

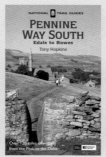

PENNINE WAY SOUTH
Edale to Bowes
Tony Hopkins

Over 120 miles of walking
from the Peak to the Dales

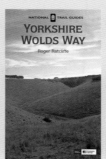

YORKSHIRE WOLDS WAY
Roger Ratcliffe

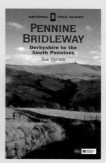

PENNINE BRIDLEWAY
Derbyshire to the
South Pennines
Sue Viccars

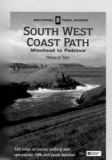

SOUTH WEST COAST PATH
Minehead to Padstow
Roland Tarr

160 miles of coastal walking with
spectacular cliffs and sandy beaches

SOUTH WEST COAST PATH
Padstow to Falmouth
John Macadam

Over 160 miles of walking on
the spectacular Cornish coast

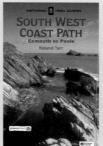

SOUTH WEST COAST PATH
Exmouth to Poole
Roland Tarr

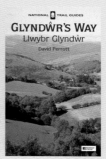

GLYNDŴR'S WAY
Llwybr Glyndŵr
David Perrott

Definitive guides to some of Britain's most popular long-distance walks

The London Loop
David Sharp

The walker's M25 – over 140 miles of
footpaths in London's secret countryside

ISBN 978 1 84513 521 8

The Coast to Coast Walk
Martin Wainwright

The classic high-level walk
from Irish Sea to North Sea

ISBN 978 1 84513 560 7

The Capital Ring
Colin Saunders

78 miles of green corridor
encircling inner London

ISBN 978 1 84513 568 3

West Highland Way
Anthony Burton

Ninety-three miles of Scottish moor
and mountain in Britain's most
spectacular long-distance walk

ISBN 978 1 84513 569 0

Published by **A**urum